FAMILY PRAYERS.

FAMILY PRAYERS

BY THE AUTHOR OF

"*MORNING AND NIGHT WATCHES,*" etc.

Sixty-seventh Thousand.

NEW YORK
HENRY FROWDE
91 & 93 FIFTH AVENUE.

Our Father,
Which art in Heaven,
Hallowed be Thy Name. Thy
kingdom come. Thy will be done in
earth, As it is in Heaven. Give us this day
our daily bread. And forgive us our
trespasses, as we forgive them that
trespass against us. And lead us
not into temptation; but deliver
us from evil: For Thine is
the kingdom, the power,
and the glory, for
ever and ever.
Amen.

CONTENTS.

Occasional Prayers.

First Week.

SUNDAY MORNING.

ALMIGHTY GOD, we desire to approach Thy sacred presence, thanking Thee that Thou hast permitted us to see the light of another day of the Son of man. This is the day which the Lord hath made; we will rejoice and be glad in it. Draw Thou near to us, as we draw near to Thee. Inspirer of all good thoughts, do Thou pre-occupy our hearts with Thyself. May we walk in the light of Thy countenance.

Thy favour is life. Nothing but the possession of Thine infinite love can satisfy the longings of our souls. Whom have we in heaven, O GOD, but Thee? and there is none upon earth we would desire besides Thee.

We acknowledge our unworthiness; the depravity and corruption of our nature; the sins and shortcomings of our practice. We have to mourn over unrequited kindness, resisted warnings, unimproved providences, neglected privileges. For the sake of JESUS CHRIST, the Son of Thy love, have Thou mercy upon us, miserable offenders! We bring our guilt to the Great Propitiation. We bring the burden of daily transgression to the Lamb of GOD, who taketh away the sin of the world. In Him, receive us graciously and love us freely. Hidden in the clefts of the smitten Rock, may it be ours to take up the song of the pardoned, "O Lord, we will praise Thee; though Thou wast angry with us, Thine anger is turned away, and Thou comfortest us: Behold, God is our salvation: we will trust, and not be afraid: for the Lord Jehovah is our strength and our song, He also is become our salvation."

Lord, subdue within us whatever is inconsistent with Thy mind and will. Put a sanctified restraint on our thoughts; repress all vain imaginations; crucify every remaining sin. May our hearts become holy temples, and our lives living sacrifices. Let eternity exercise a more commanding influence over us, and religion become more "the one thing needful." May we grow in meek and childlike submission to our Heavenly Father's will. Breathing a perpetual Sabbath-spirit on earth, may we be fitted for that rest which shall never be broken, which awaits Thy people in the Kingdom of the Redeemed.

We pray for those who are this day to minister to us in the sanctuary. Give them an unction from the Holy One. May every impression of Thy Holy Word be rendered permanent and saving. May we be in the Spirit on Thy day, and enabled to pitch our tents near the gate of Heaven. Bless any who may be prevented waiting along with us in the courts of Zion. May they that tarry at home divide the spoil; and know that Thou art not confined to temples made with hands.

Bless us a family and household. As we are knit together in earthly ties, do Thou unite us in the better bonds of the everlasting covenant. Make us partakers of the resurrection-life of Thy people; that, though death may sooner or later separate us here, we may meet at last where separation is unknown. We commend all belonging to us to Thy sovereign care. May the pillar of Thy presence go continually before them. Give them the heritage of those that fear Thy name.

We pray for the poor, the afflicted, the bereaved, and the dying. O Thou Comforter of all that are cast down, do Thou heal their sorrows, bind up their wounds. To the friendless, do Thou prove a Friend. In the multitude of their thoughts within them, may Thy comforts delight their souls.

Hear us, gracious God, for the sake of Him whom Thou hearest always, and in whose most precious name and words we would further pray, saying,

Our Father, &c.

The grace of our Lord, &c.

SUNDAY EVENING.

HEAVENLY FATHER, we desire to close Thy holy Sabbath, looking up to Thee for a blessing. Thou hast been as a pillar of cloud before us this day; Thou hast again spread for us a table in the wilderness; we have again seen Thy glory, as we have seen Thee heretofore in Thy Temple. As the shadows of night are falling around us, do Thou, the "Sun of our Souls," be near us—dispersing the darkness of sin, and giving us the inner sunshine of Thy presence and love.

We entreat Thee graciously to forgive the many sins that have mingled in our efforts to serve Thee. If we were to be judged by our holiest seasons, how should we stand condemned! Look not on us as we are in ourselves; but behold our shield;—look on the face of Thine Anointed. We would cleave to Him as our only Saviour. Enable us to testify the reality of our faith, by bringing forth the peaceable fruits of righteousness. May Thy love reign paramount within us; may there be no competing affection. May we seek to show by our pure lives and consistent walk, that we have been imbibing the Saviour's Spirit. Take these unworthy, erring hearts; sanctify and seal them for Thyself; make them Thine;—Thine only, and Thine wholly, and Thine for ever. Clothe us with the armour of righteousness; enable us to exercise a holy jealousy over ourselves, lest things temporal should tend to exclude things eternal. May it be our great aim to be progressing in the Divine life. Let us ever hear Thy voice saying, "Arise, and depart ye, for this is not your rest!" May our habitual response be, "We desire a better country,—that is an Heavenly."

We pray for a world lying in wickedness. How long shall the wicked—how long shall the wicked triumph? Save Thy people, and bless Thine inheritance, feed them also, and lift them up for ever. Bless abundantly the preaching of Thy holy word. Glorify Thyself in the salvation of sinners. May the hands of Thy ministering servants be made strong by the arms of the mighty God of Jacob; may bows, this day, drawn at a venture, have carried the arrow of conviction or of comfort to many hearts.

We entreat Thee to take under Thy protection all our beloved friends. It is our privilege to bring them in prayer to the Mercy-Seat. Though unable to meet within the same sanctuary, it is our comfort to know that no distance can estrange from Thee;—that Thou canst, at one and the same moment, be present within every gate of Zion and every dwelling of Jacob. We commend both present and absent ones to the gracious Shepherd of Israel. Be Thou to them as the shadow of a great rock in a weary land.

Draw near to the sons and daughters of sorrow. Give them everlasting consolation and good hope, through grace. Let them bow to Thy will. Let them see no hand in their trials but Thine; saying, in lowly submissiveness — The Lord gave, and the Lord hath a sovereign right to take away.

We thank Thee for Thy many mercies still vouchsafed to us. Watch over us during this night. Grant us the sleep of Thy beloved; and when we awake, may we still be with Thee. And all that we ask is in the name and for the sake of Jesus Christ our only Lord and Saviour; to whom, with Thee, the Father, and Thee, O Eternal Spirit, one GOD, be ascribed all blessing, and honour, and glory, and praise, world without end. *Amen.*

Our Father, &c.

The grace of our Lord, &c.

MONDAY MORNING.

O LORD, we desire to draw near into Thy gracious presence, in the name of Him whom Thou hearest always, and in whom Thou art ever well pleased.

Give us grace to approach Thee, under a deep sense of our unworthiness. We have nothing to plead in extenuation of our guilt. We have sinned against light and privilege, warning and mercy. We mourn our deep-rooted depravity, our constant proneness to depart from Thee; the feebleness of our faith, the coldness of our love, the imperfection of our best services, the mingled motives in our holiest duties. We come anew, casting ourselves on the infinite fulness of our adorable Redeemer. In Him is all our hope. Give us, out of His inexhaustible treasury, even grace for grace. Transform us into His image. May we seek to walk in His footsteps, and to copy His example; bearing continually about with us the dying of the Lord Jesus, may the life also of Jesus be made manifest in our mortal flesh.

O God, let it be our constant aim and endeavour to know what Thy will is; and may we have strength given us to obey it. May we cheerfully submit to whatever Thou seest meet to appoint. May we murmur at nothing that brings us nearer Thee. Conscious of the supreme enthronement of Thy love in our hearts, may we be enabled to avow, "LORD, Thou knowest all things, Thou knowest that we love Thee." Loving Thee supremely, take what Thou wilt away, we must be happy.

GOD of Bethel, dwell in this household; make every member of it a member of the household of faith. Bless all our friends. Those that are absent, LORD be near them. Those that are in distress, LORD comfort them. Those that know Thee not, LORD reveal Thyself unto them. Those that are Thy children, do Thou increase their devotedness.

Prosper Thy cause and kingdom everywhere. Let Satan's kingdom be destroyed —the kingdom of grace advanced—the kingdom of glory hastened. Give to each of us this day Thy gracious benediction; and when our days on earth are finished, may it be ours to spend the years of Eternity in the full vision and fruition of Thee, our GOD, through JESUS CHRIST our only Lord and Saviour. *Amen.*

Our Father, &c.

The grace of our Lord, &c.

MONDAY EVENING.

O GOD ALMIGHTY, who hast mercifully shielded us during another day, we desire, ere we retire to rest, to commit ourselves, soul and body, to Thee in well-doing, as unto a faithful Creator. Glory be to our GOD for all the blessings of the light; and now that the curtain of evening is again drawn around us, do Thou keep us beneath the shadow of Thy wings. It is Thou, Lord, only, who makest us to dwell in safety.

We acknowledge Thee as our daily Benefactor and Guardian. Thine is the air we breathe, the food we eat, the raiment with which we are clothed. But far above all Thine other gifts, we bless Thee for JESUS, the Son of Thy love. He is our only Saviour. We would exult anew, in the assurance, that His blood cleanseth from all sin; and that He is able to save to the uttermost. We rejoice to think that He is at this moment pleading in behalf of His people;—the "Wonderful Counsellor;"—the Prince who has power with God, and must at all times prevail.

May we be clothed with His Spirit, as well as with His righteousness. Make us like Him, patient and meek, thankful and forgiving. Take away all pride, vainglory, and hypocrisy—all absorbing love of the world. Set our affections on things above; and enable us to pass through things temporal, so that finally we lose not the things that are eternal.

May we seek to be zealous in the performance of our relative duties. Let us feel that whatever talents Thou hast given us, are trusts to be laid out for Thy glory, and to promote the well-being of those around us. Whatsoever our hand findeth to do, may we do it with our might.

Visit Thy church—the vineyard which Thine own right hand hath planted. May grace, and mercy, and peace be upon the Israel of GOD. Bless our own household; may every heart within it be given unto Thee. Let none of us leave for a dying hour, what may be best done, and it may be, only done, now. May all our friends at a distance enjoy the friendship of an ever-present God. Guard them, guide them, provide for them. May we walk together the same Zionward path; and at last have an abundant entrance ministered into that better land, where Thou shalt rest in Thy love, and rejoice over Thy people with singing. Hear us, for the sake of Thy dear Son, our only Lord and Saviour, who, when He was on earth, taught us thus to pray, saying,

Our Father, &c.

The grace of our Lord, &c.

TUESDAY MORNING.

O LORD, Thou art from everlasting to everlasting, God. Thou inhabitest the praises of eternity: Thy glories no time can impair; Thy mercy endureth for ever. Who shall not fear Thee and glorify Thy name, for Thou only art holy!

We bless Thee for the Son of Thy love. We rejoice that for every sinner casting himself on His fulness and sufficiency there is a gracious welcome. Reposing on His completed work, we can triumphantly say, 'Return unto Thy rest, O our souls, for the LORD hath dealt bountifully with us.'

O God, enable us to *enter* into this rest. Forbid that we should delay availing ourselves of Thine offered mercy. May every other question be subordinated to this, "What must we do to be saved?" May we know that JESUS is in every respect the SAVIOUR we need. Let us experience the blessedness of living *with* Him in holy fellowship, *upon* Him with unfaltering dependence, and *to* Him in undivided consecration of soul and body. Enable us to search out the plague of our own hearts. Laying aside every weight, and the sin that doth more easily beset us, may we run with patience the race that is set before us, looking unto Jesus. May whatever pleases Him please us. May we find all our happiness in the inquiry, 'What the will of the LORD is;' and knowing it, let us joyfully pursue our heavenward way. While thankfully employing the manifold gifts of Thy bounty,—O God, keep us from the abuse of any, by allowing them to supplant the Giver. May they be hallowed and sanctified to us by connecting them with Thyself—Thou Source and Bestower of all!

Bless all in sorrow. Descend, LORD, to heal their wounds. May they bow with unrepining submission to Thy will, and say, 'It is good for us that we have been so afflicted!' May those laid on beds of languishing, manifest patience under bodily pain and infirmity, glorifying Thee in the furnace-fires. May useful lives be spared, and the dying be prepared for death.

Hasten the promised times of refreshing from the presence of the LORD. May JESUS take to Himself His great power and reign. Let the day soon come, when He shall have dominion from sea to sea, and from the river unto the ends of the earth, when all kings shall fall down before Him, and all nations shall serve Him. Restrain human passion. Scatter the people that delight in war. Give peace in our time, O God, for there is none other that fighteth for us, but only Thou, O God.

Bless this family and household: may we all know the happiness of the Shepherd's fold. [May the lambs of the flock be gathered in His arms and carried in His bosom.]

Take us this day under thy peculiar care. The LORD bless us and keep us —the LORD cause His face to shine on us — the LORD be gracious unto us and give us peace, for JESUS' sake. *Amen.*

Our Father, &c.

The grace of our Lord, &c.

TUESDAY EVENING.

O GOD, we come into Thy blessed presence this evening, anew to thank Thee for the unmerited tokens of Thy love and mercy. On Thee we are dependent for all the temporal bounties of our lot, and for all our higher and more enduring spiritual privileges. If we have been enabled this day to resist temptation, and to fight against sin, it is Thy grace which has enabled us to do so. We are weak, and helpless. Our hearts are ever dealing treacherously both with ourselves and Thee. The good that we would, that we do not; and the evil that we would not, that we do.

Nothing else but the merits of our blessed Redeemer can save us. We take refuge in the fulness of His grace—in the completeness of His finished work. Our souls would magnify the Lord, our spirits would rejoice in God our Saviour; for He that is mighty hath done great things for us, and holy is His name.

And while we look by simple faith to His atonement, as the alone ground of our justification, we would look to The HOLY SPIRIT to work in us all the good pleasure of His goodness. May He mould us after the Saviour's image, and conform us to His will,—enabling us to live under the sovereignty of that lofty motive, to walk and act so as to please Jesus. Lord, give us supreme love to Thee; fervent charity to all men; faithfulness to whatever trust Thy Providence has confided to us. May we seek to live, as we would wish we had been living, when we come to a dying hour.

Have mercy on the sons and daughters of sorrow. Let them own Thy hand; let them rest in Thy love. Let them rejoice in Him who is the Brother born for adversity; and if they see not the bright light in the cloud, may they trust Thine own promise, "At evening time it shall be light."

Promote Thy cause and kingdom in the world. Pour out upon Thy ministers, and missionaries, and churches, the healthful Spirit of Thy grace. May the time soon come when all the ends of the earth shall see the salvation of GOD.

Bless our own immediate dwelling, and the circle who are nearest and dearest to us. May the peace of God, which passeth understanding, keep their hearts. Number them with Thy saints in glory everlasting.

Be with us throughout this night. May our bodies be refreshed with sleep; and may we awake to the duties of a new day with our minds stayed on Thee. And unto Thy great name, FATHER, SON, and HOLY SPIRIT, we ascribe blessing, and honour, and glory, and praise, now and for ever. *Amen.*

Our Father, &c.

The grace of our Lord, &c.

WEDNESDAY MORNING.

O GOD, Thou art great, and greatly to be praised: Thy greatness is unsearchable. Thou art the GOD of our life, and the length of our days; Thou appointest our lot, and settlest the bounds of our habitation. The Lord reigneth. Nothing befalls us but what is the dictate of infinite wisdom and everlasting love. How unvarying has been Thy kindness. We have to tell of mercy upon mercy; and there are no small mercies with Thee. All Thy mercies are great, for the least of them are undeserved.

We thank Thee especially for that mercy which transcends all others in magnitude: we bless Thee for a full and everlasting salvation in JESUS. May we be justified freely by His grace. May He be formed within each of us the hope of glory. May we be enabled, with some good measure of triumphant confidence, to say,—We know whom we have trusted, and we are persuaded that He is able to keep that which we have committed to Him against the Great Day.

Anew this morning, as thy Redeemed children, we would present our souls and bodies as living sacrifices to Thee. May we feel this to be a reasonable service. May all that is displeasing to Thee be disowned: may new-born principles ripen into holy tastes and permanent habits. May we add to our faith, virtue, and knowledge, and temperance, and patience, and godliness, and brotherly kindness, and charity. May all anger, and wrath, and malice, and evil speaking be put away from us; remembering Him who was meek and lowly in heart,—who when He suffered He threatened not, but committed Himself to Him who judgeth righteously.

LORD, be Thou our covenant God. Thy presence hallows all joy, sweetens all sorrow, and takes the sting from every thorn and every cross. If we have Thy favour and blessing, we are independent of every other. Heart and flesh faileth, but Thou art the strength of our heart and our portion for ever.

We pray for the afflicted. Be a father to the fatherless—a husband to the widow—the stranger's shield—and the orphan's stay. Let every heavy-laden one know that it is *Thy* gracious hand that appoints every burden. Give us all grace to be resigned to Thy will. May this be the only breathing of our hearts, "Father, glorify Thy name!"

[Do Thou sanctify our home. May our children rise up and call Thee blessed! Pour Thy rich grace early into their hearts; may they be led to remember their Creator in the days of their youth. May this be esteemed their highest privilege—that they are the children of their Father in Heaven.]

Hasten, LORD, Thy kingdom. Bring in Thine ancient people with the fulness of the Gentile nations. Prosper the labours of Thy missionary servants; may the LORD stand by them and strengthen them. May they not be afraid of evil tidings; may their hearts be fixed, trusting in the Lord.

May each of us feel that in our several spheres we have some work to perform for Thee. Let the solemn word of warning be ever sounding in our ears, "The night cometh wherein none of us can work." Oh, may we be diligent, that we may at last be found of Him in peace, without spot and blameless; and all that we ask is for the Redeemer's sake. *Amen.*

Our Father, &c.

The grace of our Lord, &c.

WEDNESDAY EVENING.

O GOD, we desire to come into Thy presence on this the close of another day. We beseech Thee to fill our souls with some befitting conceptions of Thy greatness,—Thy divine majesty and glory.

What mercy it is in Thee to bend Thine ear to our feeble lispings of praise, and to listen to the pleadings of such unthankful unholy hearts. We could not have ventured to approach Thy footstool, but for Thy great love in CHRIST JESUS. Through Him alone it is, that the words of our mouths and the meditations of our hearts are rendered acceptable in Thy sight. In Him we are pardoned, justified, adopted, saved. In Him we are kept, sanctified, sealed. In Him we shall at last be presented without fault before Thy throne.

Blessed Saviour, we may well intrust our eternal all to Thy keeping. Our wants are infinite, but our help in Thee is infinite. Thou art waiting to dispense needed grace, and for every time of need. LORD, we feel that we require grace for everything; there is not the hour or moment we can live independent of Thee. Carry on Thine own work within us. Hold Thou us up, and then alone we shall be safe. May the fruits of righteousness abound in us. Purge us, that we may bring forth more fruit. Forbid that we should be content to remain sapless, unproductive cumberers, occupying ground in Thy vineyard, but yielding no revenue of glory to Thee. This is Thy will concerning each of us, even our sanctification. Oh! Thou who searchest Jerusalem with candles, do Thou search our hearts; see if there be any wicked way in us, and lead us in the way everlasting. Lead us not in our own way. Often would we choose what would be detrimental to our best interests. But choose Thou for us. Let us rejoice in Thee as a rich Provider, and an all-wise Provider; who will give us nothing, and deny us nothing, but what is for our good.

We commend to Thy protection all near and dear to us this night. Keep them, gracious Father, under the shadow of Thy wings; bless them and make them blessings. May they never lose sight of the chief end of their being,—to glorify Thee on earth, and to enjoy Thee for ever in Heaven. Bless our own family. We thank Thee for all Thy great goodness in the past. The LORD hath been mindful of us, and He will bless us.

Do good in Thy good pleasure unto Zion. Build Thou the walls of Jerusalem. May every branch of Thy Church universal be blessed with tokens of Thy favour. Revive Thy work, O GOD, in the midst of the years.

Take the charge of all of us this night; it is Thou who givest Thy beloved sleep; it is Thou, LORD, only, who makest us to dwell in safety. Spare us, if it be Thy will, to see the light, and to enjoy the comforts of another day. And all that we ask is for the Redeemer's sake. *Amen.*

Our Father, &c.

The grace of our Lord, &c.

THURSDAY MORNING.

MOST BLESSED GOD, Thou hast again permitted us to see the beginning of another day. We desire to accept every new morning as a fresh gift of Thy love. We are the constant dependents on Thy bounty. If Thy sustaining arm be withdrawn, we instantly perish.

We are unworthy to come into Thy presence. There is nothing so amazing as Thy condescension towards us. Thou mightest righteously leave us to perish in our sins, and make us the monuments of Thy displeasure. But in the midst of deserved wrath Thou art remembering unmerited mercy.

We come to Thee through the new and living way of access. We cast ourselves on the full, free, and everlasting salvation of our adorable Redeemer. Our souls would magnify the Lord: our spirits would rejoice in God our Saviour, for He that is mighty hath done great things for us, and holy is His name. Blessed be the Lord God of Israel, for He hath visited and redeemed His people, and hath raised up for us an horn of salvation in the house of His servant David. May each of us have a personal and a saving interest in all those covenant blessings which He died to purchase, and which He lives to bestow. May we take Him as ours only —ours wholly—ours for every step Zionwards—ours till we reach the gates of glory,—yea, ours for ever and ever! Grateful to Thee, O God, for all Thy goodness to us in the past, we desire to commit ourselves to Thy guidance for the future. It is our blessed consolation that no good thing wilt Thou withhold from them that walk uprightly. We will hear Thy voice behind us saying, "Fear not, for I am with thee." "Be still; and know that I am God."

LORD, impress us with a sense of the value of time. May we seek to make the most of the present fleeting hours, while they are still our own. Let us live under the power of holy principles; that so, when called to give an account of our stewardship, we may do so with joy and not with grief.

Bless all near and dear to us. Our friends we commend to Thy friendship. Let not one of them be found wanting on the Great Day. May the Eternal GOD be their refuge, and underneath them the Everlasting Arms.

Compassionate those in sorrow. May all poor afflicted ones take refuge in the assurance that Thou art the GOD of Providence; that whatever befalls them is Thy doing; and that the sunshine of Thy countenance can make up for every loss. Spare useful and valued lives. Unto the Lord our God belong the issues from death. Sanctify us now before Thee, in body, soul, and spirit: seal us unto the day of eternal redemption. We ask these, and all other blessings, for the sake of Jesus Christ, Thine only Son our Saviour, to whom, with Thee the

Father, and Thee, ever blessed Spirit, be ascribed all praise and honour and glory, now and ever. *Amen.*

Our Father, &c.

The grace of our Lord, &c.

THURSDAY EVENING.

O GOD, we desire to come into Thy blessed presence, thanking and praising Thee for the renewed experiences we have enjoyed of Thy faithfulness and love. Another day of mercy and grace has been added to those which have preceded it. We rejoice to look back on the way by which Thou hast hitherto led us; protecting us from danger, supporting us in trouble, disappointing our fears, and realising our hopes. We bless Thee for our creation, for our preservation, for all the blessings of this life; but above all, for Thine inestimable gift, JESUS the Son of Thy love. Enable us this evening, like the believing suppliant of old, to touch by faith the hem of His garment, and to receive the benediction, "Your sins are forgiven you: go in peace." We would seek to draw fresh supplies from the fountain of His grace; knowing that He is equal for all exigencies; and that there is a fulness in Him to meet all wants and minister to all necessities.

It is our desire, blessed GOD, to lie passive in Thy hands. Whether prosperity or adversity be ours, whether Thou chasten us or gladden us, oh bring us nearer Thyself. Save us from the bitterest of all trials, the removal of Thy love—the loss of Thy favour. Strengthen us for duty: guard us from temptation: and enable us so to pass through things temporal, that finally we lose not the things that are eternal.

When we cannot understand Thy dealings, may faith repose in Thine unchanging faithfulness. May we feel assured that all things are working together for our good; and that what is mystery here, will be unfolded and unravelled hereafter. Now, we see through a glass darkly, but then face to face. Meanwhile, may we walk less by sight and more by faith. May we live under the powers of a world to come: and be looking for that blessed hope, even the glorious appearing of the Great God our Saviour.

[Take each and all of our family under Thy special guardianship. Thou Better than the best of earthly parents, be the guide and protector of our children. May they be the children of the living GOD. May their hearts be early given to Thee; and by holy and obedient lives, may they glorify their Father in Heaven.]

We pray for Thy cause and kingdom everywhere. Give Thy Son the heathen for His inheritance, and the uttermost parts of the earth for His possession. May He take to Himself His great power, and reign. May there soon be voices heard saying, The kingdoms of this world are become the one Kingdom of our LORD and of His CHRIST.

LORD, all our desires are before Thee; all our hope is in Thy mercy, all our happiness is in Thy favour. Abide with us, for it is toward evening, and the day is far spent; and when our evenings and mornings shall merge into everlasting day, be Thou still our All in all; for the sake of JESUS CHRIST, Thine only Son, our Saviour. *Amen.*

Our Father, &c.

The grace of our Lord, &c.

FRIDAY MORNING.

O LORD, we adore Thee as GOD over all, blessed for evermore. Thou art the former of our bodies and the Father of our spirits; the GOD in whom we live, and move, and have our being. All we are, and all we have, is derived from Thee. There is nothing we possess that we have not received. Oh give us grateful hearts; feeling that the least blessing we enjoy, is unmerited on our part, and a gift of free grace on Thine.

We come anew, glorying in the work and merits of our adorable Surety. Thou art in Him waiting to be gracious, not willing that any should perish. May the unwavering eye of faith be kept, Blessed Saviour, on Thee, and on Thy completed salvation. We have nothing to pay, Thou hast *paid* all. We have nothing to procure, Thou hast *procured* all; everlasting forgiveness, everlasting righteousness—union and communion with Thee now and evermore. To Thee we look for everything. Save us from every false confidence. Elevate our affections: purify our desires: make us more heavenly minded. Let us, while living in the world, live above it. Let Thy Spirit be our teacher; let Thy word be our guide; let Thy will be our sovereign motive; let Thy glory be our ultimate end. May we make religion more the one thing needful. Let us not remain content with an indefinite hope of final safety. Pilgrims and strangers on the earth, may we declare plainly that we seek a better country.

Give us a salutary sense of the uncertainty of life. May we feel that the great secret of existence is to be in habitual preparedness for a dying hour. We know not what may be before us. Oh to be living so, that the step between us and death may be a step between us and glory.

Bless all connected with us by whatever tie. May we be able to love all our friends in Thee. May there be bonds uniting us together which will survive the uncertain ones of earth. We commend to Thy special care those who are absent. May an ever-present GOD be with them. Guide them by Thy grace; defend them from temptation; fit them, by the salutary dealings of Thy providence, for the varied duties of the present life, and for the joys of Thy Heavenly Kingdom.

Bless the lambs of Thy flock. [More especially those now before thee.] We commend them to the Great Shepherd of the sheep, beseeching Him to bring them early to His fold, and to make them perfect to do His will. We put ourselves, blessed GOD, in Thy hands. May all our doings this day, begun, carried on, and ended in Thee, redound, through JESUS, to Thy praise and glory. And all we ask is for His sake. *Amen.*

Our Father, &c.

The grace of our Lord, &c.

FRIDAY EVENING.

O LORD our GOD, we desire to bow this night at the footstool of Thy Throne, adoring Thee for all Thy great goodness. What are we that we should be permitted to come into Thy presence, or take Thy thrice blessed name into our sinful and polluted lips? Thou hast not dealt with us after our sins, but according to Thy rich and undeserved mercy.

Thou art the Author of our being, and the source of all that makes existence joyous and happy; Thy favour alone is life. Bereft of Thee, we are bereft indeed.

Enable us to *feel* our sins,—to have a deep and heartfelt consciousness of their heinousness in Thy sight. We are apt to cloak and dissemble them; we are reluctant to make a frank and unreserved confession of them all. LORD, give us grace, in true penitence and contrition of heart, to cast ourselves, *un*worthy, on the infinite worthiness of Him who is *all-worthy*. For His sake, receive us graciously—love us freely. We rejoice to meditate on the love which He had for us from all eternity. We rejoice to think that it is the same at this hour that it was then,—unchanging, everlasting. O Thou great Angel of the covenant, do Thou accept of these our unworthy petitions: perfume them with the incense-cloud which ascends continually from Thy hand. Sanctify us, body, soul, and spirit. Make us altogether what Thou wouldst have us to be. Let us be willing, if need be, to deny ourselves and take up our cross and follow Thee. May we be among the number of those who follow the Great Captain of their Salvation whithersoever He sees meet to guide them. Strong in the LORD, and in the power of His might, may we go on our way rejoicing.

Bless Thine own cause and kingdom everywhere. LORD, how long shall the wicked, how long shall the wicked triumph? Save Thy people, and bless Thine inheritance; feed them also, and lift them up for ever. We would look forward to that time when earth shall become one consecrated temple,—when every day shall be a Sabbath,—every heart an altar,—every tongue praise,—and JESUS CHRIST owned as LORD, to the Glory of GOD the Father.

God of Bethel—Thou GOD of all the families of the earth, who hast promised to show mercy to thousands of them that love Thee,—do Thou bless our household, and give to us the heritage of those that fear Thy name. [Bless our children; may they early know those ways which are pleasantness, and those paths which are peace. May they be enabled, by Thy grace, to resist temptation, and to beat down Satan under their feet.] Bless young and old, master and servants. Let none of us be left to seek for the first time a living Saviour at a dying hour. But laying hold of Him now, may we be found at last unto praise and honour and glory at His appearing and Kingdom.

We would retire to rest this night, reposing in Thy gracious providence, —beseeching Thee, if it be Thy will, to spare us to see the light and to enjoy the comforts of a new day; and all we ask is in the name and for the sake of JESUS CHRIST our only Saviour. *Amen.*

Our Father, &c.

The grace of our Lord, &c.

SATURDAY MORNING.

MOST BLESSED GOD, whose nature and whose name is Love; we, Thy dependent creatures, desire to draw near this morning to the footstool of Thy throne. Vouchsafe us, we entreat Thee, Thy presence and blessing. We would begin the day with Thee. We would enter on all its duties supplicating Thy favour; feeling that Thy favour is life, and that all the happiness the world can give, cannot compensate for its loss.

We approach with deep humility. LORD, we are vile, what shall we answer Thee? Ours is not only the guilt of rebels, but the ingratitude of children. We have abused the care and the kindness of the best and most beneficent of Parents. We have too often *known* our doings to be sinful, and yet we have persevered in them. We have too often *known* what was in accordance with Thy will, and yet we have not followed it

We have reason to marvel that Thou hast borne with us; that Thou hast not, long ere now, consigned us to the doom of the cumberer.

We would look away from ourselves, to Thy dear Son, our Redeemer; feeling that if we are saved it must be by Him alone. May He be formed within us the Hope of Glory. By His grace and Spirit, may we be brought under the power and influence of renewed affections. Let us seek to manifest the reality of our union with Him, by bringing forth all the peaceable fruits of righteousness,—adorning the doctrine of GOD our Saviour. May ours be an active and devoted obedience. Expel from us whatever is unholy. Let us live as the expectants of a glorious immortality. Lord, may we habitually remember, that here we are Pilgrims. Oh be Thou our constant Guide in all our journeyings. Let us never go but where Thou directest: let us never hesitate when and where Thou callest us. Let us not arraign the allotments of

Thine infinite love. May we feel that all the circumstances of life—its joys and its sorrows—its comforts and crosses—are ordained by Thee in adorable wisdom. Our way might have been hedged up with thorns, but it has been full of mercy. Thou hast *been* our help, leave us not, neither forsake us, O God of our salvation. Give us to see written over every hour of the future, "So shall Thy strength be."

Bless all near and dear to us. Defend our friends by Thy mighty power. Surround them with Thy favour as with a shield, and bring them at last to the enjoyment of Thine immediate presence. Bless especially those now before Thee. [May our children be the objects of Thy love, and the subjects of Thy grace; may they be enabled to say, 'Our Father, Thou shalt be the guide of our youth.'] We commend each and all of us this day to Thy keeping. Let us enter upon its duties with our souls stayed on Thee. And all that we ask is in the name and for the sake of the LORD JESUS, in whose name and words we would further call Thee—

Our Father, &c.

The grace of our Lord, &c.

SATURDAY EVENING.

O GOD ALMIGHTY, Thou Sovereign Proprietor of the Universe, do Thou bow Thine ear to the voice of our supplications, as on this the close of another day,—when another week of mercy is receding,—we venture to approach the Throne of the heavenly grace. Father, we have sinned against Heaven and in Thy sight, we are no more worthy to be called Thy children. Long ere now mightest Thou have turned away Thy face from us, and our prayer from Thee. We are wonders to ourselves that we are still spared. What guilt on our part,—yet what forbearance on Thine! What aggravated ingratitude on our part,—yet the LORD waiting to be gracious and willing to pardon! What sins against privilege, —slighting Thy warnings—grieving Thy Spirit; and yet for all this, Thy hand of mercy is stretched out still!

We desire to remember how it is

we are still permitted to approach Thy footstool. It is through the Son of Thy love; for His work's sake—His obedience and righteousness' sake. But for Him, we must have been for ever without GOD and without hope. We plead anew His finished atonement. We would glory in nothing but His cross. Give each of us to enjoy the blessedness of the assurance that there is no condemnation to them that are in Christ Jesus. Let us not rest, until, with personal, appropriating faith, we can say, "We know whom we have believed, and we are persuaded He is able to keep that which we have committed unto Him."

May Thy HOLY SPIRIT take of the things that are CHRIST'S, and show them unto our souls. May He touch us as with a live coal from off the altar: purifying our affections, elevating our desires; making our hearts living temples, with this as their superscription, "Holiness unto the Lord." If led often to mourn over our dulness, and coldness, and lukewarmness here, may it be ours, O GOD, to look forward to that day, when there shall be nothing to mar the joy of entire and undivided consecration to Thy service.

Bless our beloved friends both near and at a distance; may they all be near to Thee. May there be no separation between them and Thy favour. Any who are in sickness, Lord, succour them. Any who are in bereavement, Lord, comfort them.

Pity a careless, ungodly world,—arrest the spread of impiety,—establish the reign of purity and righteousness. Give us grace to be faithful among the faithless; resolving that, whatever others do, as for us, we will serve the LORD.

Be with us this night. Watch over us as we sleep. May night after night of refreshing slumber, be to us the emblem of that better rest above, when, in perfect security, we shall dwell in the house of the LORD for ever. Prepare us for the services of Thy day. Attune our minds for its sacred duties. May each recurring Sabbath, as it brings us nearer Eternity, find us better prepared for it; and all that we ask is for the Redeemer's sake. *Amen.*

Our Father, &c.

The grace of our Lord, &c.

Second Week.

SUNDAY MORNING.

MOST GRACIOUS GOD, who hast in Thy good providence again permitted us to see the light of Thy Holy Day, do Thou draw near to us in Thy great mercy. Thou hast dispersed the darkness of another night; may the Sun of Righteousness arise upon us with healing in His beams. May our fellowship be with the Father and with His Son JESUS CHRIST.

We thank Thee for the stated return of this season of sacred rest, when, away from the feverish anxieties of earth, we may give heed to the things which concern our everlasting peace.

We bless Thee for the great truth which this day more especially commemorates.

We bless Thee that JESUS has burst the bands of the grave, and triumphed over principalities and powers. The LORD is risen! He hath satisfied all the demands of Thy holy law; He hath finished transgression, made an end of sin, made reconciliation for iniquity, and brought in an everlasting righteousness. The LORD is risen! He hath fully vanquished our foes; Satan's power is overthrown, and the kingdom of heaven is opened to all believers.

We take refuge anew at the foot of His cross, bringing infinite unworthiness to infinite merit and all-sufficiency. Wash us, blessed Saviour, in the fountain opened for sin and for uncleanness: receive us graciously: love us freely. Being made free from sin, and having become the servants of God, may we have our fruit unto holiness and the end everlasting life. LORD, give us grace ever to walk as the heirs of immortality. Let us bear about with us the recollection that time is short. Let us live as if each Sabbath might possibly be our last. May a sacred spirit pervade this day's services. May we glean from these, for the week on which we have just entered, what will form a preservative against the world's snares, and dangers, and temptations.

We pray for those who dishonour Thy Day and profane Thy holy name; who reject the offers of Thy grace, and continue in alienation and sin. Ere the door of mercy is for ever shut, do Thou turn them from their wickedness; point them to JESUS, and show them that "neither is there salvation in any other." Unfold to them the fearfulness of meeting Thee as they are, unpardoned and unreconciled. Let them know the preciousness of that precious assurance, "He is able to save unto the uttermost."

Thou Source of all consolation, draw near to the afflicted. Abundantly sanctify Thy dealings. Stay Thy rough wind in the day of Thy east wind. May this thought silence every murmur, "He that spared not His own Son, but freely gave

Him up for us all, how shall He not with Him also freely give us all things."

GOD of Bethel, do Thou bless all related to us by the bonds of earthly affection. May they evermore have affiance in Thee. Shepherd of Israel,—Thou who leadest Joseph like a flock,—may they be safe under Thy gracious guidance, and repose in Thy love. [Bless our children. Pour Thy rich grace into their hearts. Let them not fall a prey to the allurements and enticements of a present evil world, but may they walk as seeing Thee, who art invisible.]

Bless Thy holy Church throughout all the world. Clothe Thy priests with salvation: let Thy saints shout aloud for joy. Own, this day, Thine own appointed instrumentality in the preaching of the everlasting Gospel. May Thy word prove quick and powerful, sharper than a two-edged sword. It is not by might, nor by power, but by Thy Spirit, O Lord God of Hosts.

Let Thy mercy, O GOD, be upon us,

according as we hope in Thee; and when our Sabbaths on earth are ended, may ours, at last, be an unending Sabbath in Thy presence and favour. And all that we ask is in the name and for the sake of Him whom Thou hearest always, and to whom with Thee, the Father, and Thee, O Eternal Spirit, one GOD, be ascribed, all blessing and honour, and glory and praise, world without end. *Amen.*

Our Father, &c.

The grace of our Lord, &c.

SUNDAY EVENING.

ALMIGHTY and EVERLASTING GOD, we desire to draw near to the footstool of Thy throne of grace, thanking Thee for all the mercies of the past day. We will set up our Ebenezer of gratitude, and say, "The LORD hath helped us." We bless Thee that Thou hast permitted us once more, on earth, to enjoy the rest and quiet of Thy holy Sabbath; that again we have been invited to hush worldly disquietudes and cares, and have our minds stayed on Thee. Pardon whatever Thou hast seen amiss in our attempts to serve Thee. May our persons and our services be accepted in the Beloved. May they be perfumed with the fragrance of His adorable merits.

We desire anew this night to repair to His cross. We disown all trust in ourselves. Other refuge, other righteousness, we *have* none, and we *need* none. We cleave, in simple dependence, to the work of JESUS. We are safe only when clinging to the horns of the blood-besprinkled altar. LORD, give us to know the happiness of being at peace with Thee through Him. Every blessing, temporal and spiritual, we would desire to connect with Thy favour. Every rill of creative, providential, and redeeming mercy, we would trace to Thyself, its great fountain-head. Every cross and loss we would submit to, as the appointment of Thy wisdom. The roughest path we would tread, if Thou leadest us there!

May all Thy dealings toward us issue in our sanctification. May our hearts be becoming holier and better. Transform us more from day to day, and from week to week, into the image of Thy Son; that we may at last be presented faultless before the presence of His glory with exceeding joy.

We pray for all who may have worshipped with us this day. May grace, mercy, and peace be upon them, and upon the Israel of GOD. Bless Thy ministering servants, more especially those who have spoken unto us Thy word. Out of the abundance of their hearts, may their lips speak; may they ever hear the sound of their Master's footsteps behind them.

Extend Thy cause and kingdom everywhere. May the glorious Gospel of the grace of God speedily triumph over all the pride, and reason, and will-worship, and delusion of man. Arise, O GOD, and plead Thine own cause. May it long be our privilege to repair without let or hindrance to the living waters of Salvation. Continue to us the bliss of unbroken Sabbaths, and quiet sanctuaries, and peaceful communions.

Bless our family. O Thou who hast brought again from the dead the LORD JESUS, that Great Shepherd of the sheep,—through the blood of the Everlasting Covenant, make us all perfect to do Thy will, working in us that which is well-pleasing in Thy sight. May we be found at last among Thy sealed ones—members of the white-robed multitude who shall "go no more out." May our friends who are at a distance from us, be protected and guarded by Thy gracious providence. The Lord watch between them and us when we are absent one from another,—may *their* names also be written among the living in Jerusalem. Teach us all to be walking as pilgrims and strangers on the earth,—sojourners as all our fathers were,—looking for that blessed hope, even the glorious appearing of the great GOD our SAVIOUR. May we pass the time of our sojourning here in fear,—prepared for whatever may be Thy will concerning us—for health or for sickness—for joy or for sorrow—for life or for death.

Have mercy on the afflicted. Let the prayer of faith save the sick. Spare useful and valued lives. Let not the Sun of life go down while it is yet day; but turn the shadow of death into the morning. Comfort the bereaved. Sustain the dying. Prepare them for their great change.

Through another night, be pleased to grant us Thy guardian care. Shepherd of Israel, may Thy wakeful, sleepless eye be upon us. May the shadows of this night's darkness be to us only as the shadow of Thy wings. Shield soul and body by Thy mighty power. Lying down in Thy fear, may we awake in Thy favour, fitted for the duties of a new day. All this we ask for the sake of JESUS CHRIST, our only Saviour. *Amen.*

Our Father, &c.

The grace of our Lord, &c.

MONDAY MORNING.

O LORD, Thou art glorious in holiness, fearful in praises, continually doing wonders. Blessed be Thy name, that though Thou art the Greatest of all Beings, Thou dost stoop to hear our prayers and listen to our wants. It is because Thou art God and not man, that we are still in the land of the living, and in the place of hope. Day by day have our sins incurred Thy righteous displeasure. We have left Thy bounty unacknowledged—Thy love unrequited. We have to tell of unthankful hearts, ungodly lives, deep corruptions. Lord, impress us with a sense of our guilt. Let us feel it is no light matter to sin against Thee, and to be living in unconcern of Thy manifold mercies. Sinners—the chief of sinners—we would look away from ourselves, to the work and merits of our Great Redeemer. Blessed Saviour, Thou art waiting to be gracious. All the mighty load of our guilt we would transfer to Thee, our adorable Surety. Thou hast already satisfied the requirements of a righteous law. As our Kinsman and Elder Brother, Thou art now within the veil; as willing, as Thou ever wast, to save unto the uttermost.

While we look to Thee as the LORD our Righteousness, may we know Thee also as the LORD our strength. May we imbibe more of Thy blessed Spirit. May we be learners at Thy feet,—learning to deny ourselves, and to bear all that Thou choosest to appoint, without a murmur: knowing that it must be for the best. May we be enabled to follow Thy footsteps and to reflect Thy purity. May Thy love animate us in the discharge of every daily duty. May we act under the feeling, "we are not our own." Consecrated soul and body to the LORD who died for us, may life become a tribute-offering to Thy praise. Preserve us from the snares of a wicked world. Strengthen us in seasons of weakness. Protect us in the hour of temptation. To us to live may it be Christ; so that when called to leave this scene of probation, we may die in peace, and have our souls filled with hopes of heaven.

LORD, bless our friends—reward our benefactors—forgive our enemies. May our household ever have Thy gracious benediction resting upon it. May every member of our family, near and at a distance, have the seal of GOD on their foreheads, and be numbered with Thy saints in glory everlasting. Pour Thy rich grace into the hearts of the young. Let them not suffer golden moments to pass by misimproved. Let them know the happiness of living under Thy continual favour.

Look in kindness on the sick, the sorrowful, the aged, the bereaved, and the dying. Accommodate Thy grace to their varied wants and trials. Let them take refuge in the mercy of Him who is chastising them; rejoicing that all which concerns them and theirs, is in Thy hands and at Thy disposal.

Hear these our humble prayers: when Thou hearest, forgive; and grant us an answer in peace, for the LORD JESUS CHRIST'S sake. *Amen.*

Our Father, &c.

The grace of our Lord, &c.

MONDAY EVENING.

MOST GRACIOUS GOD, Father of all mercies, GOD of our salvation,—we desire, this evening, to approach the footstool of Thy Throne of Grace. We would end another day of mercy with the offering of grateful hearts. What shall we render unto Thee for all Thy benefits? Never for a solitary moment hast Thou withdrawn from us Thy hand of love. We rejoice that we have such a GOD on whom to cast our cares; and who has given us, in the past, so many wondrous proofs, that "He careth for us."

We desire anew to look to the merits and righteousness of Thy dear Son. His blood has washed guilty thousands; and it is still free to us. We take refuge in the assurance, that coming unto Thee through Him, confessing our sins, Thou art faithful and just to forgive us our sins, and to cleanse us from all iniquity.

Do Thou take these hearts of ours and make them Thine. May our inmost thoughts, and desires, and purposes, be dedicated to Thy glory. May we be living as the expectants of immortality; walking worthy of Thee unto all well-pleasing, being fruitful in every good word and work. Feeling our responsibilities as the servants and stewards of Thy household, may our time and talents be more laid out for Thee, that when our LORD cometh, He may receive His own with usury.

Bless all the family of the afflicted. GOD of all consolation, do Thou bind up their wounds. Keep them from a hasty spirit, under dark dispensations. Let them know and believe that infinite love is in all Thine arrangements; that finite wisdom has no place in Thy chastisements; that He with whom they have to do, cannot do wrong. LORD, give us all this lowly spirit of submission to Thy will. Whether Thou chasten us, or gladden us, whether prosperity or adversity be our portion, oh bring us nearer Thyself. May Thy dealings serve to trim the lamp of faith and keep it brightly burning.

Extend Thy covering wings over all whom we love. May none of our friends be unbefriended by Thee. Bless our own immediate household;—sprinkle its lintels with the covenant token. [Write the names of servants and of children in the Lamb's book of life.] May each of us at last be included in the invitation, "Come, ye blessed of my Father, inherit the Kingdom prepared for you from the foundation of the world." May our lives now be hid with CHRIST in GOD, that when CHRIST, who is our life, shall appear, we may also appear with Him in glory.

Regard with favour Thy Church everywhere. Thou hast promised abundantly to bless Thy Zion and to satisfy her poor with bread. We pray for the peace of Jerusalem. They shall prosper that love Thee. Scatter the darkness that is now brooding over the nations. Arise, O GOD, and plead Thine own cause.

Watch Thou over us during the unconscious hours of sleep. May we close our eyes at peace with Thee, and awake refreshed and invigorated for the duties of a new day.

Hear these our unworthy petitions; and when Thou hearest, forgive, and grant us an answer in peace, for the Redeemer's sake. *Amen.*

Our Father, &c.

The grace of our Lord, &c.

TUESDAY MORNING.

O GOD, Thou art the KING of Kings, and LORD of Lords. We draw nigh unto Thee, this morning, rejoicing that we have a Throne of Grace, to which, through the merits of Thy dear Son, our only Saviour, we can ever repair. Ere we enter on the day's duties, may a shower of heavenly blessing descend to refresh our souls. If we are blest by Thee, we must be blessed indeed.

We confess our great unworthiness:—our sins of thought, word, and action;—our sins of omission and commission;—our sins against light and privilege, warning and mercy.

We repose every burden upon Him who hath "borne our griefs and carried our sorrows." Blessed JESUS, we would dismiss all our own misgivings, and cast ourselves on Thy promised grace and strength. We rejoice in Thee as "GOD only wise;"—mighty to save: to whom all power has been committed in Heaven and in Earth. Thou doest all things well, and nothing but what *is* well. Enable us to rely on Thy guiding arm, and to merge our wills in Thine. Hold Thou us up, and we shall be safe.

O GOD, forbid that, in the midst of earth's cares and pursuits, we should ever lose sight of our immortal destinies. Let us imbibe more of the pilgrim spirit; having our eye upwards, and our footsteps onwards. Let us not forfeit fleeting opportunities. In every providence may we hear, as it were, an angel's voice saying, 'Why sleep ye? arise! let us be going;—the night is far spent, the day is at hand.' May each of us in our varied spheres be led to ask, 'LORD, what wouldst Thou have me to do?' Let us all seek to do *something* for Thee. If we are forbidden to do much in the way of active service, may we endeavour to manifest the power of a holy life, and to leaven our daily duties with Thy fear.

Bless the members of this household. May they walk before Thee with a perfect heart. [May the young be enabled to adorn the doctrine of GOD their Saviour in all things. May the servants be enabled to act from the lofty motive,—"We serve the LORD CHRIST."]

Bless our native land. Bless all in authority. May the time soon come, when the crowns and sceptres of the earth shall be cast at the feet of Him who is KING of Kings and LORD of Lords. Hasten the day, when the wilderness and the solitary place shall be made glad, and the desert shall rejoice and blossom as the rose.

We commend ourselves, O God, to Thee. Guide us—provide for us—go before us. Let us have the conscious assurance that Thou art for us, and then none can be against us. We have no care of our own, we cast our cares upon Him who careth for us. Prepare us for whatsoever Thou hast in store for us. For joy or for sorrow; for health or for sickness;

for living or for dying. And all we ask is for the LORD JESUS CHRIST'S sake. *Amen.*

Our Father, &c.

The grace of our Lord, &c.

TUESDAY EVENING.

O LORD, we desire to draw near to the footstool of Thine Eternal Throne. We bless Thee for all the renewed proofs we have had, during another day, of Thy care and kindness. While others have been pining in sickness, laid on beds of languishing and death — we are still among the living to praise Thee. Oh may the lives preserved by Thy bounty, be dedicated to Thy praise.

Far above all Thine other gifts, we bless Thee for Thine inestimable love in the redemption of our world by the LORD JESUS, for the means of grace and for the hopes of glory. We bless Thee that Thy well-beloved Son has brought in an everlasting righteousness; —that He has magnified Thy law and made it honourable:—that He has dispelled the darkness of the Valley of Death; and opened the gate of Heaven to all believers.

We desire to make acknowledgment of our unworthiness and guilt. We will not cloak nor dissemble our manifold and multiplied transgressions. Discover to us the depths of our depravity ; unveil to us the secret pride and selfishness and worldliness of our hearts. Deliver us from our besetting sins. Let us see their vileness in the cross of Thy dear Son. May the power of sin wax weaker and weaker : may the power of Thy grace within us wax stronger and stronger. May our souls become living altars, and our lives living sacrifices. Yielding our members as instruments of righteousness unto holiness, may we serve Thee in newness of spirit.

LORD, we know the proneness of the heart to put off the solemn consideration of the one thing needful. Many have lived with good intentions, and yet have perished. Let it not be so with us. Let us not be slumbering and sleeping. Let us not be among the number of presumptuous ones, who are saying, "The LORD delayeth His coming." May we be ever ready, ever watching; having the girded loins and burning lamps, so that when the summons shall be heard, "Behold, the Bridegroom cometh," we may be ready with the response, "Lo! this is our GOD, we have waited for Him."

May the seal of Thy covenant mercy be on all now before Thee. [Master and servant, parents and children, young and old.] May every night, as it gathers around us, remind of the approach of the long night of death; and may it lead us to think of the awaking time in that glorious morning, when, in the full vision and fruition of Thee, our GOD, earth's shadows and darkness shall for ever flee away.

Bless the aged; may Thy favour and love rest on the hoary head as a crown of glory. Bless the young; may they early know what are alone the ways of pleasantness and the paths of peace. Bless the afflicted—the bereaved—the solitary—the forsaken—the dying; may they know Him who hath said, "I will never leave thee, nor forsake thee."

Give us all grace to trust Thee implicitly, even when Thy dealings cross our own purposes and frustrate our wills. Let us obey no will but Thine. Following Thy guiding footsteps, may we say, "The LORD is our Shepherd, we shall not want."

Watch over us, blessed LORD, this night. May Thy good angels encamp round about us. Give us refreshing sleep, even the sleep of Thy beloved; may we lie down to rest in Thy fear, and awake in Thy favour. And all that we ask is in the name of Him who, while He was on earth, taught us thus to pray, saying,

Our Father, &c.

The grace of our Lord, &c.

WEDNESDAY MORNING.

O GOD ALMIGHTY,—KING of Kings and LORD of Lords. Thou art the Maker, Proprietor, and Judge of all. We approach Thee as our Covenant GOD and Father; trusting in the name and merits of our adorable Redeemer. What mercy it is that we have such a refuge to repair to! that amid our own faithlessness we can ever repose in the faithful saying, "that JESUS CHRIST came into the world to save sinners." We renounce all dependence on ourselves. Wretched, and miserable, and poor, and blind, and naked—we take Him as all our salvation and all our desire.

We are no judges of what is good for us; what blessings are best to receive—what mercies are best withholden. We would often seek what is not for our well-being; but we rejoice in the infinite wisdom and tenderness manifested in Thine allotments. Let us ever feel, regarding each and all, "This also cometh from the Lord of hosts." May we seek in every providence to hear Thy voice,—in every event to read Thy will. May we live conscious of the predominating motive of love to Thee. May we feel Thy favour lightening every cross and lessening every care. LORD, give us more of the simplicity of children. Keep us watchful, and humble, and thankful. Keep us from pride and vain-glory; from envy and uncharitableness; from evil surmisings and unkind insinuations; from all that would exalt us at the expense of others. May we learn to esteem others better than ourselves.

Look in great mercy on the family of sorrow; be their support and consolation: and teach us all, in the midst of health and strength, to prepare for the hour of adversity. There is nothing permanent here. May we know what it is to look to a strong tower which cannot be shaken. We are in our true rest if we are in Thee. Do Thou gladden our pathway through life. May we be lighted through the dark Valley with the lamp of Thy love; and enjoy through eternity Thy beatific presence.

GOD of Bethel, we commend our family, and all related to us by whatever tie, to Thy care. Seal to them an interest in the everlasting covenant. [Bless the young. May they know the happiness of those who fear Thee. Great Shepherd of the sheep, preserve them from the snares of a world lying in wickedness. May they be early taught of GOD, and so inherit Thine own promise to such—"Great shall be the peace of Thy children."]

Take us under Thy care this day. May all our duties be gladdened with a sense of Thy presence and love. May we have a single eye in all we think, and say, and do, to the glory of Him, in whose most precious words we would farther pray—saying,

Our Father, &c.

The grace of our Lord, &c.

WEDNESDAY EVENING.

O ETERNAL, EVERLASTING GOD, Fountain of all happiness, GOD of all grace, we desire this evening to acknowledge anew with grateful hearts Thine undeserved mercies. Thou hast made our cup to overflow with blessings. From the very threshold of our being, Thou hast been our Protector and Guardian. Thou hast shielded us from unknown dangers—Thou hast warded off unseen calamities;—no earthly friend could have loved us and cared for us like Thee.

We bless Thee for the liberty of access we enjoy at all times into Thy sacred presence; to make known our varied wants, and to ask for mercy to pardon and for grace to help in every time of need. We need everything; but Thou hast promised in JESUS, Thine own dear Son, to make us perfect and entire, wanting nothing. Helpless, hopeless, friendless, portionless by nature, we cast ourselves on Him who is help and hope and friend and portion to all who seek Him. We have no trust but in His work. Sprinkle these polluted hearts with His pardoning, peace-speaking blood. Hide us in the clefts of the smitten Rock. Safely sheltered there, we can make the triumphant challenge, "Who shall separate us from the love of Christ?" We mourn our distance and estrangement from Thee; our guilty departures, our coldness and insensibility. Let Thy wondrous patience and kindness lead us to repentance. Turn Thou us, LORD, and we shall be turned; draw us and we shall run after Thee. May every thought, and affection, and feeling, and temper, be brought into captivity to the obedience of JESUS. May we love what He loves, and hate what He hates. May we know the happiness of true holiness; and experience somewhat of the joy of angels, in doing Thy holy will on earth as they do it in Heaven. Fill us with all joy and peace in believing, that we may abound in hope through the power of the Holy Ghost.

Bless our family and friends; may our household be one of the dwellings of the righteous. May every member of it be zealous in the promotion of Thy glory, remembering that the day is coming when we shall be called to give an account of our stewardship. Our moments are gliding swiftly by. Forbid that any among us should be found seeking oil when the lamp of life is going out. Do Thou, even now, LORD, from Thine own mercy-seat, replenish our empty vessels. Let us be living with a dying hour in view. Let us die daily to sin, and live daily to God; that when the hour of our earthly departure arrives, it may be to all of us the birthday of a new life, in glory everlasting.

We ask all these manifold blessings, for ourselves and for others, in the name and for the sake of our adorable LORD and Saviour, who is now within the veil;

and where, with Thee, O Eternal Father, and Thee, O ever-blessed Comforter, Three in One in covenant for our redemption, He ever liveth and reigneth, world without end. *Amen.*

Our Father, &c.

The grace of our Lord, &c.

THURSDAY MORNING.

O GOD, Thou art great, and greatly to be feared, Thy greatness is unsearchable. Another day has in mercy dawned upon us. We desire to enter on its every duty with our minds stayed on Thee. May all our doings be ordered by Thy governance; that we may be enabled to perform those things that are pleasing in Thy sight, and to promote the glory of Thy holy name.

We bless Thee for all the loving-kindness Thou hast hitherto made to pass before us. From our earliest infancy Thy protecting hand has been around us,—shielding us from unseen dangers, preventing us with the blessings of Thy goodness. And we are, this morning, once more gathered around the footstool of Thy throne, the monuments of Thy patience, and forbearance, and mercy.

We bless Thee especially for JESUS, and His great salvation. We rejoice that

He is both willing and able, and *as* willing as He is able, to save unto the uttermost: that all are alike warranted and welcome to repair to the fountain He has opened for sin and for uncleanness.

Lord, give us grace to improve our manifold privileges while we have them. Let us not remain asleep in sin,—enjoying the means of grace, yet trifling with convictions. May we "occupy" till our LORD comes,—seeking to witness for Him by the testimony of a consistent life. May this be our habitual feeling—"what manner of persons ought we to be, in all holy conversation and godliness?"

We commend to Thee all the family of affliction. Take them under Thy special protection. It is behind the cloud Thou often speakest most tenderly,—teaching precious lessons, which in no way else could be learnt. Let Thy suffering people wait till they hear the "still small voice." Calling upon Thee in the day of trouble, and experiencing Thy delivering hand, may they be led to "glorify Thee." Teach us all, in the season of health and strength, so to live, that when the night cometh, we may be enabled to resign the trust of existence to its great Proprietor,—and to say, "Now, LORD, lettest Thou Thy servant depart in peace."

Bless our beloved friends; forbid that any one of them should be found wanting on the day when Thou makest up Thy jewels. May they all be set as gems in Immanuel's crown, and be found unto praise, and honour, and glory, at His second appearing.

Bless Thy Church. Imbue her ministers and people with the healthful spirit of Thy grace. Extend everywhere the boundaries of the Redeemer's kingdom. The harvest truly is plenteous, and the labourers are few. We would pray the Lord of the harvest to send forth labourers to His harvest.

Be Thou with us, O God, this day; may the everlasting arms be underneath and round about us; may we be diligent in business, fervent in spirit, serving the LORD; and look forward with joyful hearts to that better world, where we shall have no contrariety of mind to Thee, when we shall be *with* Thee, and *like* Thee; serving Thee without distraction; and where sin and sorrow will be no more felt or dreaded. And all that we ask is for JESUS' sake. *Amen.*

Our Father, &c.

The grace of our Lord, &c.

THURSDAY EVENING.

O GOD, we bless Thee for Thy great mercy; that we are again permitted to approach the throne of the Heavenly grace. Many have been summoned this day into eternity. We have been spared. The shadows of night have again fallen around us in peace.

We thank Thee for the continuance of health and strength, and many outward blessings. We thank Thee for the crowning mercy of all—JESUS, Thine unspeakable gift. We rejoice that Thou art in Him reconciling the world unto Thyself. Thousands of needy, outcast sinners have repaired to Him, yet still the Fountain of His grace is free as ever. This is still His name and memorial—"Mighty to save."

LORD, we come to Thee, with all our demerits, casting ourselves on His infinite and all-sufficient righteousness. Wash every guilty stain away. Forgive our sins of omission and our sins of commission. May the Angel be caused to fly swiftly and touch us in this the time of our evening oblation. One day's transgressions are enough to condemn us. There is nothing but Thy sacrifice and continual intercession, O Thou Great High Priest, between us and everlasting destruction. It is Thy all-powerful grace alone which, from hour to hour, averts from us temptations we could have no strength in ourselves to resist. Hold Thou us up, and then alone we shall be safe. In all time of our tribulation—in all time of our wealth, in the hour of death, and at the day of Judgment, good LORD, do Thou deliver us.

Come forth out of Zion, and turn away ungodliness from Jacob. Instruct the ignorant—reclaim the wanderer—save the obdurate and impenitent. Convince them, ere it be too late, that there is no loss comparable to the loss of the soul,—to be left hopeless and portionless for ever! Point them to the Lamb of GOD

—cleanse them in His atoning blood—and make them the monuments of Thy mercy.

Look down in kindness on all who are in affliction. Draw near to those who may be bereaved of near and dear friends; be Thou to them better than the name of Son or Daughter, or any earthly relative;—may they know that He is faithful that promised—"*I* will never leave thee nor forsake thee."

Bless all our beloved friends; write their names in the Lamb's Book of life; may the pillar of Thy presence go before them night and day continually.

Bless our own family; may every name be set in the breast-plate of the Great High Priest. [Bless our children; may they all be taught of the Lord, and great shall be their peace.] Bless the servants; may they walk before Thee with a perfect heart, and as seeing Him who is invisible.

Take the charge of us during the silent watches of the night; when we awake, may we awake to praise Thee, and to use the powers and the talents committed to us, to Thy glory. And all that we ask is for the sake of JESUS CHRIST, our blessed LORD and SAVIOUR. *Amen.*

Our Father, &c.

The grace of our Lord, &c.

FRIDAY MORNING.

OUR FATHER, who art in Heaven, what are we, sinful dust and ashes, that we should be permitted, morning after morning, to take Thy name into our lips? We bless Thee for all the unmerited proofs of Thy kindness. From our earliest years we have been the recipients of Thy bounty. With all a Father's tenderness Thou hast watched over us. We *have* received, and we are still receiving, of the LORD'S hand "double for all our sins."

We draw near in the name of Him whom Thou hearest always. "Nothing in our hands we bring,"—we would cling "simply to His cross." Empty us of all self-righteousness;—let us feel our deep creature-destitution;—let us stand alone in the finished righteousness of the All-righteous One. We have forfeited all claim to Thy favour. We have turned aside like a deceitful bow;—and if we had been left to our own treacherous hearts and wayward wills, we must long ago have perished.

We desire to look to Thy grace in the future. There is not a corruption we have within us which that grace is unable to subdue; there is not a cross or trial, or care, but it will enable us to endure. Whatever Thy leadings may be, let us cheerfully confide in their wisdom and faithfulness. We are poor judges of what is good for us, but we can trust Thee in all things;—in what is great and what is small, what is dark and what is bright, what is joyous and what is grievous. We rejoice that all is in Thy hands, and all is for the best. May we ever regard sin as our greatest trial. When temptation assails us, grant us power to resist it. May our conversation, our tempers, our affections, our desires, be regulated by the example of our divine LORD and Master. Give us His meekness of spirit, which no provocation could ruffle,—His forgiveness of injuries amid ingratitude and scorn,—His calm, unmurmuring submission to thy holy will.

Bless all the sons and daughters of affliction. Let them view every dark providence as an errand of love in disguise,—a messenger sent from the Eternal Throne, to minister to them who are heirs of salvation. May we all live as pilgrims on the earth. Make us meet for the time when our earthly work and warfare shall cease, and when, in unspotted sanctity, we shall stand without fault before the Throne.

LORD, take the charge of each and all of us. Vouchsafe to keep us this day without sin. May all our doings be ordered by Thy governance, to do that which is well-pleasing in Thy sight, through JESUS CHRIST our only LORD and SAVIOUR. *Amen.*

Our Father, &c.

The grace of our Lord, &c.

FRIDAY EVENING.

O GOD, we desire to draw near into Thy sacred presence, thanking Thee for the mercies vouchsafed to us during another day. Many of our fellow-men have, since its commencement, passed into eternity, their season of grace fled for ever. We are still spared. The living—the living—we shall praise Thee, as we do together this night.

We bless Thee especially for the tokens of Thy mercy in JESUS. We bless Thee for His full, free, everlasting Redemption. Oh set us in the Clefts of the Rock, and hide us there. Let us feel the all-sufficiency and security of His covenant love. That for infinite want there is infinite fulness,—that for infinite danger there is an infinite salvation.

LORD, give us grace to live worthy of our high calling. Enable us to adorn the doctrine of our GOD and SAVIOUR. Let His love be the animating principle in our actions. Let our chief delight be to serve Him—our greatest pain to vex and grieve Him. May our affections be more elevated—our eye more single—our lives more consistent—religion more the one thing needful. May we rest in the confident persuasion that Thou dost all things well, and nothing but what *is* well. Enable us to exercise a child-like acquiescence in Thy dealings. These may at times be mysterious; but when Thy purposes of love are at last unfolded, we shall dwell with adoring gratitude on all the way by which Thou hast led us. Give us grace, meanwhile, to be living as dying creatures. Let us never forget our pilgrim character, nor dream away, in guilty unconcern, our fleeting moments.

Look in kindness on this household; may they all have the rich and enduring heritage of those that fear Thy name. [Bless the children; may they be taught of GOD.] Bless the servants; may they serve the LORD CHRIST, doing justly, loving mercy, and walking humbly with

Thee their God. Bless all our absent friends. Be Thou ever present with them. If there be any still at a distance from Thee, LORD, bring them nigh, through the blood of the everlasting covenant. Let not one be found wanting at the Great Day.

We pray for the Church universal. O Thou Great High Priest, do Thou feed every golden candlestick with the oil of Thy grace. Be Thou the "all in all" of every church, as of every believer. Do Thou promote union among Thy true people. Let them not live apart, looking coldly and distantly on one another. Feeling that they are all one in CHRIST JESUS, may they love one another with a pure heart fervently; and thus the Church on earth may be a dim reflection of the glorious Church of Thy redeemed in Heaven.

Watch over us during the silence and darkness of another night; and spare us, if it be Thy will, to see Thy light, and to enjoy the comforts of another day.

Hear these our humble supplications. And all that we ask is for JESUS' sake *Amen.*

Our Father, &c.

The grace of our Lord, &c.

SATURDAY MORNING.

ALMIGHTY GOD, we desire to come anew this morning into Thy sacred presence. Glory be to Thy holy name, that we are again permitted to draw near to the footstool of Thy Throne, and to call Thee "Our Father." Our pillow last night might have been a pillow of death. We might have found ourselves this morning righteously exiled from Thy presence,—knowing Thee only as "the consuming fire." But Thou hast lengthened out our day of grace. We are still among the living to praise Thee. It is of the LORD'S mercies that we are not consumed.

Anew we draw near to the opened fountain;—anew, gracious Saviour, we plead Thy spotless merits. It was Thine own errand of wondrous love,—that which brought Thee from Thy Throne in Heaven,—to proclaim liberty to the captives, and the opening of the prison to them that are bound. Do Thou usher us into the glorious liberty of Thy people. May we feel that there is no real happiness independent of Thee;—that all else are walking in a vain show—seeking rest but finding none. But if Thou make us free, we shall be free indeed. Enable us to take Thee as the strength of our hearts and our portion for ever.

Keep us from the absorbing power of earthly things. Let us not be dead to Thee, and alive only to a dead and dying world. Let not the seen and the temporal eclipse the higher and nobler objects of faith. May we live under the powers of a world to come,—loving Thee now with some feeble and imperfect foretaste of that love with which we trust we shall love Thee for ever.

We rejoice to believe that we are entirely in Thy keeping. If Thou sendest us prosperity, LORD, hallow it. If Thou sendest us adversity, LORD, sanctify it. May all things work together for our good.

We commend to Thy gracious providence those in whom we are more specially interested. Take our friends under Thy peculiar care. Sanctify them by the indwelling of Thy Holy SPIRIT;—prosper them outwardly and inwardly;—may all their duties and occupations be leavened with godliness. Bless our own immediate circle:—may GOD be our Father, and JESUS our elder Brother, and Heaven our everlasting home. [Bless our children—defend them from a present evil world. Let them early know the happiness of seeking and finding the one thing needful.] Bless the servants; may they fulfil the duties of their calling, not with eye-service as men-pleasers, but doing the will of GOD from the heart.

May Thy kingdom come. Support and strengthen all devoted labourers in heathen lands. May Thy Spirit come down as rain upon the mown grass—as showers that water the earth. Sanctify affliction to all in sorrow. Let Thy suffering people rejoice in the assurance that

Thy chastisements are the dealings of a Father; that the furnace is lighted to purge away the dross, and refine and purify for glory.

Direct, control, suggest, this day, all our thoughts, purposes, designs, and actions, that we may consecrate soul and body, with all their powers, to the glory of Thy holy name. And all that we ask or hope for, is for the Redeemer's sake. *Amen.*

Our Father, &c.

The grace of our Lord, &c.

SATURDAY EVENING.

O LORD, we desire to approach Thy Throne of Grace this evening, adoring Thee as GOD over all, blessed for evermore. Draw near to us as we draw near to Thee. We bless Thee that Thou hast spared us during another day, and another week. Let us end every day and every week as if these might possibly be our last; as if the midnight cry might break upon our ears, ere we see another rising sun, or a returning Sabbath.

We come, acknowledging, that it is of the LORD'S mercies we are not consumed. We *are* nothing and we *have* nothing. By nature and by wicked works we could *expect* nothing, but indignation and wrath, tribulation and anguish. Each day is a witness against us. We confess our proneness to depart from Thee the living GOD,—our reluctance to render to Thee the tribute of our undivided homage and love.

LORD, we bring our sins and lay them on Him, who, as our Surety Substitute, was wounded for our transgressions, and bruised for our iniquities. We bring our weakness to His Almighty strength; we bring our insufficiency, that we may receive from Him, the promised "all-sufficiency in all things." We rejoice, blessed Saviour, to think of Thee, as sympathising with us in all our trials and perplexities and temptations;—keeping us as the apple of Thine eye, and feeling what is done to Thy people as if it were done to Thyself. Enable us to repose in the infinite fulness of Thy grace and mercy; to experience the blessedness of an unreserved, unwavering trust and confidence in Thy dealings. Let us confide to Thee the allotment of all that befalls us. Let us harbour no suspicions of Thy faithfulness and love. Let us commit the unknown morrow to Thy better wisdom, saying, "Teach us the way wherein we shall walk, for we lift our souls unto Thee."

O GOD, while we pray for ourselves we would remember before Thee all whom we ought to bear on our spirits at a Throne of Grace. Prosper Thy cause and kingdom in the world. Bring the wickedness of the wicked to an end: may the Prince of Peace take to Himself His great power and reign. Bless the young; may they spring up as willows by the water-courses: may they be trees of righteousness, the planting of the LORD. Bless the aged; may they be gathered into the garner of the Great Husbandman, as the shock of corn in its season;—full of years and ripe for glory.

Bless all Thy faithful ministers—especially those who, to-morrow, are to proclaim Thy holy word;—strengthen them outwardly and inwardly, as they go forth, bearing the precious seed; and on the great reaping-day of judgment, may they come again with rejoicing, bringing their sheaves with them. Bless us as a family; —master and servant, [parents and children.] Let us all own one common Master —one Father in Heaven.

Be with us throughout the silent watches of the night. Whether we wake or sleep, may we live together with Thee. There is no darkness to us if Thou art with us. Defend us during the unconscious hours of slumber, that we may rise on Thy Holy Sabbath fitted for duty, happy in the assured continuance of Thy favour and love. And all we ask is for JESUS CHRIST'S sake. *Amen.*

Our Father, &c.

The grace of our Lord, &c.

Third Week.

SUNDAY MORNING.

ALMIGHTY and EVERLASTING GOD, we bless Thee for the return of another day of the Son of man. We thank Thee that we have been spared during another week, while many of our fellow-men have been called to render in their account. Give us filial nearness to Thee our Father in Heaven. Let us hear Thy gracious benediction—"Peace be unto you." May Thine own Day be begun, carried on, and ended, under a sense of Thy presence and favour. May all worldly thoughts, and cares, and disquietudes, be laid aside, that we may enjoy a foretaste of the everlasting blessedness which is at Thy right hand.

We come, gracious LORD, relying on Thy mercy and love in JESUS. We would direct the undivided eye of faith to His finished salvation; rejoicing that it is as free as ever, and as efficacious as ever. Fill us with a deep and humbling sense of our guilt. May we mourn an erring past, and receive grace for an unknown future. We would seek this day anew to enkindle our love at Thy holy altar. Inspire us with resolutions of new obedience. May we no longer live unto ourselves—to the world—to the creature—to sin. May the great Creator and the adorable Redeemer occupy, without a rival, the throne of our affections. Let us cultivate a holy fear of offending Thee. Let us no longer continue in guilty estrangement, forfeiting Thy favour and our own true happiness. May the love of God be shed abroad in our hearts, by the Holy Ghost, given unto us.

We desire to remember in Thy presence, all in whom we are interested. Bless Thy people, this day, throughout the Christian world; may multitudes be added to the Church, of such as shall be saved. Strengthen Thy ministering servants;—may they have singleness of eye, and singleness of aim, in the proclamation of Thy holy word. May many careless souls be arrested; may weak ones be strengthened; may sorrowing ones be comforted; may the weary and heavy-laden obtain rest. May a Sabbath-spirit follow us all throughout the week; and may this day—the memorial of the Saviour's Resurrection—be to us also an earnest of the everlasting rest which remains for Thy people in glory.

We commend our dear friends especially to Thy protection. May they, too, be in the Spirit on the LORD'S day; may they call and find the Sabbath a delight. Keep them, good LORD, by Thy mighty power. May they live soberly, and righteously, and godly, in this present world; looking for that blessed hope, even the glorious appearing of the great GOD our SAVIOUR. Bless the members of our family circle; keep them ever near to Thee. [May our children be the peculiar care of the great and good Shepherd. May they know early the safety and happiness of His fold; make them to lie down in the green pastures; lead them by the still waters.]

Sanctify trial to the sons and daughters of affliction. May they bow in submission to Thy sovereign appointments, saying, "Even so, Father! for so it seems good in Thy sight."

LORD, take the charge of us; and when Thy will concerning us on earth is completed, take us to dwell with Thyself in glory everlasting; and all we ask is for the Redeemer's sake. *Amen.*

Our Father, &c.

The grace of our Lord, &c.

SUNDAY EVENING.

PRAISE waiteth for Thee, O GOD, in Zion, and unto Thee shall the vow be performed. O Thou that hearest prayer, unto Thee shall all flesh come. Thou never hast said unto any of the seed of Jacob, Seek ye my face in vain. Thy thoughts to us are unchanging thoughts of love. It is of the LORD'S mercies that we are not consumed.

We approach Thee on this the evening of Thy holy Day, acknowledging our great unworthiness. Fill us with a deep sense of our guilt. We have not the humbling consciousness we ought to have of our exceeding vileness. We are apt to ourselves, if not to Thee, to plead vain excuses for our sins.

Forgive us, O LORD,—forgive us all, for Thy dear Son's sake. Wash these crimson and scarlet stains away, in the fountain opened for sin and for uncleanness. Let us know more and more the preciousness of the faithful saying, that "JESUS CHRIST came into the world to save sinners."

Enable us to live as Thy redeemed children. As He who hath called us is holy, so may we be holy in all manner of conversation. Put Thy fear in our hearts;—not the fear of torment, but the child-like fear of offending so kind a Father—so gracious and forgiving a Saviour. Blessed LORD, make these unworthy hearts of ours Thy temple;—holy altars of gratitude and love. May our lives form a continued thank-offering for Thy manifold mercies. May we count it our highest privilege, as well as our sacred duty, to walk so as to please Thee; ever maintaining the attitude of waiting and expectant servants, who are seeking to "occupy" till their LORD comes. Keep us from inactivity and sloth. Let our loins be girded and our lamps burning. Let us be growing in faith and love—in charity and meekness—rejoicing in hope of the glory of GOD.

Father, glorify Thy name. Darkness is still covering the lands, and gross darkness the people. May the time to favour Zion, yea, the set time, speedily come. Revive Thy work in the midst of the years;—in wrath do Thou remember mercy.

We pray for all in affliction. O Thou who art the healer of the broken-hearted, the comforter of all that are cast down —do Thou impart to every sorrowing, bereaved spirit, Thine own everlasting consolations. Thou art seated by every furnace. May all Thy suffering people come forth as gold tried in the fire; and so be found at last unto praise and honour and glory at the appearing of JESUS CHRIST.

We commend our family and household to Thy care. GOD of Bethel, GOD of our fathers, the GOD and Father of our LORD JESUS CHRIST, be Thou the covenant GOD of all near and dear to us. Whether they be now present or absent, may they all be near and dear to Thee. Keeper of Israel, be Thou their Keeper; guide them, guard them, sanctify them; use them for Thy service here, and bring them to the enjoyment of Thyself hereafter.

Take us under Thy providential care this night. May no unquiet dreams disturb our repose. When the gates of the morning are again opened, may it be to hear Thy benediction and blessing—"Fear not, for I am with thee." And all that we ask is for the sake of Him whom Thou hearest always; and to whom, with Thee, the Father, and Thee, O blessed Spirit, one GOD, be everlasting praise, honour, and glory, world without end. *Amen.*

Our Father, &c.

The grace of our Lord, &c.

MONDAY MORNING.

ALMIGHTY GOD, we desire, on this the morning of a new day, to approach the footstool of Thy Throne of grace. Thou art glorious in Thy holiness, fearful in praises, continually doing wonders. Thine eternity no finite mind can fathom: Thy purposes no accident can alter: Thy love no time can impair. We adore Thee as the God of our life; moment by moment we are dependent on Thy goodness; if Thou withdrawest Thy hand, we perish.

And yet, O LORD, we have not been living habitually mindful of Thee. We have too often taken our blessings as matters of course. We have had unthankful spirits in the midst of daily tokens of unmerited mercy. Above all, we have been living in guilty forgetfulness of Thy dear Son. We have not been remembering as we ought, that but for Him and His wondrous grace, we must have perished everlastingly. We have not felt, as we ought, the attractive power of His cross. Other lords have had dominion over us. The love which ought to have reigned paramount has been displaced by other affections. We have been "minding earthly things;" too often careful, and troubled, and concerned, about what will perish with the very using.

LORD, have mercy upon us. Melt our hard and obdurate hearts: renew them by the indwelling of Thy gracious Spirit. Give us henceforth a more ardent ambition to serve Thee. May we seek to exhibit now the evidences of that spiritual life begun, which will issue in the joys of eternity. All our hope is in JESUS. Help us, blessed SAVIOUR, else we die! Give us to see the adaptation of Thy character and work to all the wants and weaknesses—the trials and difficulties—the sorrows and sins of our fallen and suffering and tempted natures. There is infinite merit in Thee to meet all the magnitude of infinite guilt. May we exhibit more willingness to renounce all dependence on ourselves, that Thou mayest be enthroned in our hearts, as Lord of all. Make us more heavenly-minded—more pilgrim-like. Our graces are feeble—LORD, sustain them. Our affections are lukewarm—LORD, revive them. Search us—try us—lead us; use what discipline Thou seest best: may it all result in our growing sanctification,—in endearing to us Thy favour, and bringing us to live under a more constant and realising sense of the things which cannot be shaken, but remain.

We commend to Thee all near and dear to us. May they be shielded by Thy providence, and sanctified by Thy grace. Let them repose in the plenitude of Thy promises, and feel that to be spiritually-minded is life and peace. Bless our own family,—preserve us by Thy mighty power. May we all feel that it is Thou, LORD, only, who makest us to dwell in safety.

We put ourselves, this day, and ever,

at Thy disposal. May the everlasting arms be around us for good;—guiding through life—through death—till we are safe in glory;—through JESUS CHRIST, our only LORD and SAVIOUR. *Amen.*

Our Father, &c.

The grace of our Lord, &c.

MONDAY EVENING.

O LORD, our Heavenly Father, by whose good providence we are spared from day to day, do Thou enable us to come this night into Thy presence, with hearts filled with gratitude and thankfulness for all Thy mercies. We would be deeply humbled on account of our unworthiness. What are we, that we should be permitted to take Thy name into our polluted lips? We have sinned, what shall we say unto Thee, O Thou preserver and Redeemer of men? We have erred and strayed from Thy ways like lost sheep; we have followed too much the devices and the desires of our own hearts unto evil. We have been rebellious, and wayward, and selfish, and unthankful. We have been living in the enjoyment of countless blessings without any due acknowledgment of Thy giving hand. Thy kindness has too often been abused, Thy grace resisted. We have been worshipping and serving the creature more than the Creator, who is GOD over all, blessed for evermore.

Lord, we flee anew to the clefts of the Smitten Rock;—hide us there, from that wrath and everlasting condemnation which these our manifold sins have justly merited.

What encouragement we have to trust Thy love and mercy! We can fear no evil when Thou art with us. We rejoice that we are in Thy hands;—that all that concerns us and ours is at Thy disposal. Enable us to rest, in calm composure, in Thine infinite wisdom. Give us lowliness and gentleness; kindness and unselfishness. May our own wills be merged in the higher will of our Father in Heaven. Whatever be the discipline Thou employest, may we meekly submit to it. May we watch all Thy varied teachings, and get profit and sanctification out of them all. May they bring us nearer Heaven and nearer Thee.

Bless our household;—unite us, as a

family, in the bonds of peace. May the Blood of the everlasting covenant be sprinkled on the portals of every heart. [We commend our children to Thy care; beseeching Thee early to instil the dew of Thy grace into their souls, and to preserve them from all danger and sin.] We pray for our native land. Bless our Queen. Bless all rulers, and judges, and senators; may they be a terror to evil-doers, and a praise to them that do well. Bless the ministers of the everlasting Gospel; may they be workmen needing not to be ashamed, rightly dividing the word of truth. Whatever, O GOD, our station in life may be, may we seek to do something for the glory of Thy Holy Name; and may we feel that Thy service is self-rewarding and self-recompensing. Give us grace to work while it is called to-day. May our loins be girded and our lights burning; may we be like those who are waiting for their LORD when He returns from the wedding, that when He cometh and knocketh, we may be ready to open to Him immediately. Watch over us during this night. Grant us refreshing rest;—and spare us, if it be Thy will, to see the light of a new day. And all that we ask is for the sake of Him whom Thou hearest always, and to whom, with Thee, the Father, and Thee, ever blessed Spirit, one GOD, be ascribed everlasting praise, honour, and glory, world without end. *Amen.*

Our Father, &c.

The grace of our Lord, &c.

TUESDAY MORNING.

O LORD, we desire to draw near into Thy blessed presence on this the beginning of a new day. Do Thou accept of our morning sacrifice. Enkindle our souls with a live coal from the inner sanctuary. Throughout the day may our minds be stayed on Thee. May a sense of Thy favour and love be intermingled with all its duties, hallowing all its pleasures, and softening all its trials. LORD, we have received our being from Thy hands;—may the lives imparted by Thee, and sustained by Thee, be consecrated to Thy praise. May we feel the happiness of Thy service, and regard nothing that this world can give, as comparable to the enjoyment of Thy friendship and love.

We thank Thee, above all, for the provisions of the everlasting covenant. Gracious SAVIOUR—Thou Shepherd —Guide—and Portion of Thy people, give us the assured sense of pardon and forgiveness through the blood of the Cross. May we have no trust in anything but in Thy matchless work. May simple faith be followed by holy obedience. May we know the blessedness of a holy life; of affections once alienated from God, now alienated from the world. May no spiritual foe be permitted to obtain the victory over us; no idol to usurp Thy place in our souls. May we have strength given us either to perform or to endure Thy will, and to cleave unto Thee with full purpose of heart.

We pray for all mankind; visit, in mercy, the dark places of the earth, which are still the habitations of cruelty. Strengthen Thy Missionary servants. Arouse Thy churches to greater zeal in the promotion of Thy cause. We would pray the LORD of the harvest that He would send forth labourers to His harvest.

GOD of our fathers, be our covenant

GOD. Dwell in this family and household: hallow every heart as an altar to Thy praise. Impress upon us all a family resemblance to the Great Elder Brother, our living Head in glory. [Pour Thy grace on the young.] Each of us is advancing nearer eternity; may we seek to be becoming more and more meet for our everlasting home. Prepare us for the blessedness of uninterrupted fellowship with Thyself hereafter.

Have compassion on all who are afflicted. Pity the houseless poor, the orphaned children, the widowed heart. O Thou, who turnest the shadow of death into the morning—do Thou console and comfort them. May they adore Thee, alike in giving and in taking away; —in the dispensing of Thy gifts, and in removing them; saying, in devout submission, "Blessed be the name of the Lord."

We commit ourselves to Thy care. May the LORD GOD this day be to us a sun and shield. May the LORD give grace and glory, and withhold from us nothing that He sees to be truly good. And all that we ask is for JESUS' sake. *Amen.*

Our Father, &c.

The grace of our Lord, &c.

TUESDAY EVENING.

O LORD our GOD, we thank Thee that we are again permitted, in the multitude of Thy mercies, to see the close of another day. We desire to end it with Thee. Ere we retire to rest, we would supplicate Thy blessing and guardian care. Make not our pillow this night a pillow of death. Give Thine angels charge over us during the unconscious hours of sleep; and when we awake, may we be still with Thee.

We adore Thee, gracious GOD, as the source of all our happiness—the Author of all our blessings. Forbid that we should suffer any created good to dispossess Thyself from the supreme place in our affections. We desire to take Thee as our chief joy: to subordinate to Thee all else beside. Guide us by Thy counsel. Thou hast been gracious to us in the past; we will trust Thee in the future. Let our one animating wish and longing be—to live, and walk, and act, so as to please Thee: and thus may each returning night, as it finds us nearer eternity, find us better prepared for the enjoyment of Thy presence for ever.

Wash out all the defilements of the day; all our sins of omission and commission. Accept of us in the Beloved. Adored be Thy name, we have in Jesus the Physician who healeth all our diseases. We stand now, as we desire to stand on a Judgment-day, clothed in His spotless righteousness.

We commend, HOLY FATHER, to Thy gracious care and providence, our family and household. May each be a member of the household of faith. Do Thou, if it be Thy will, long continue unbroken our home-circle on earth; but let our true home be above. Let the watchward of each near and dear to us be this—"We are journeying unto the place of which the LORD hath said, I will give it you." [Bless the young;

train them early for glory. Preserve them from the countless temptations of a world lying in wickedness.] We pray for the afflicted; we commend them to Him who knows their frame; who Himself having suffered being tempted, is able to succour them that are tempted.

Let Thy kingdom come. Stand by Thy Missionary servants; may they have many heathen souls for their hire; many, who shall be to them as a crown of joy and rejoicing on the Great Day.

Known unto Thee are all our wants; we leave our petitions at the footstool of Thy throne, assured that in Thee we have a rich Provider. And when the provisions of the earthly journey are needed no more, may it be ours to feed on the Bread which endureth to everlasting life. And all that we ask is in the name and for the sake of Him whom Thou hearest always; and to whom, with Thee the FATHER, and Thee,

O ETERNAL SPIRIT, one GOD, be ascribed all blessing, and honour, and glory, and praise, world without end. *Amen.*

Our Father, &c.

The grace of our Lord, &c.

WEDNESDAY MORNING.

O LORD, Thou art great, and greatly to be feared, Thy greatness is unsearchable. Who shall not fear Thee, and glorify Thy name? for Thou only art holy. Eternal FATHER, who hast loved us with an everlasting love:—Eternal SON, who did so freely shed Thy precious blood for us:—Eternal SPIRIT, who art waiting and willing to renew and sanctify—yea, to make these worthless souls of ours Temples to Thy praise;—Do Thou come to us in the plenitude of Thy love this morning, that we may feel it to be good for us to draw near unto GOD.

What are our lives, but testimonies to Divine faithfulness? We look back with gratitude and thankfulness on a wondrous past,—the mercies innumerable which have been showered upon us, and that, too, in the midst of ingratitude and sin.

Bless the LORD, O our souls, and forget not all His benefits!

Where could we now have been, but for Thy great love to us in CHRIST! On Him our every hope of pardon and acceptance is built. On His work we desire every hour to live. We rejoice that we have such a Day's-Man betwixt us, who has laid His hand upon us both; that He is now pleading for us within the veil—answering for those who cannot answer for themselves. LORD, enable us to manifest our love to Him, by a holy walk and conversation, adorning the doctrine of God our Saviour in all things. Give us a tender conscience, a broken spirit, filial nearness, purity of heart, consistency of conduct, uprightness of life. Loving Thee, our GOD, may we love also our fellow-men. Bring us under the power of renewed natures and purified affections. May all that is earthly and carnal, all that is unamiable and selfish, all that is unkind and unholy, be displaced by what is pure, elevated, lovely, and of good report. Above all, may we live under the influence of unseen realities. With our faces Zionwards, may we feel that our true home is above. Stablish our hearts with the blessed truth, that the coming of the LORD draweth nigh; that so, when the hour of death shall overtake us, it may be to us an angel whispering, "The Master is come, and calleth for thee."

Compassionate those who are in affliction; may Thy sorrowing people be enabled to trust Thee in the dark: let them look forward to that joyous period when they shall come to stand in Thy presence, and trace for themselves all the wisdom of Thy now inscrutable dealings. Have pity on the careless—reclaim the backslider—arouse the lukewarm—bring back all wanderers who may have strayed from the fold.

Bless us as a family;—give us the heritage of those that fear Thy name; may the absent know Thee as ever present;—and when earth's separations are at an end, may there be a common meeting-place for us all at last, before Thy Throne.

Be our GOD and guide this day; protect our bodies from danger, preserve our souls from sin; never leave and never forsake us. And all that we ask is in the name, and for the sake of JESUS CHRIST, our blessed Lord and Saviour. *Amen.*

Our Father, &c.

The grace of our Lord, &c.

WEDNESDAY EVENING.

MOST BLESSED GOD, we desire to approach Thy sacred presence on this the close of another day. Let our prayer come before Thee as incense, and the lifting up of our hands as the evening sacrifice. Enable us to have a realizing view of Thy Divine Majesty. Glory be to Thy Holy Name, that though Heaven be Thy dwelling-place, Thou condescendest also to make every lowly heart Thy habitation. Though Thou art the greatest of all Beings, Thou art the kindest of all, and the best of all.

We come, weak and helpless and burdened, to that cross where alone there is shelter and peace for the guilty. We will not cloak nor dissemble our manifold sins and wickedness before the face of Thee, Almighty GOD, our Heavenly Father. We would confess them with a humble, lowly, penitent, and obedient heart.

Blessed JESUS, it is our comfort to

know that there is in Thee all that is required to meet our wants. We rejoice to think of Thee as Thou now art, the unchanging Intercessor within the Veil, with all the might of infinite Godhead, and all the tenderness and pity of compassionate man. May it be ours to cleave to Thee now, and to serve Thee now, that we may not be ashamed before Thee at Thy coming. May Thy love exercise a paramount influence over us. Let it be our endeavour to show that we are Christians indeed,—living Epistles, known and read of all men. Let us be gentle, and kind, and forgiving. Let us not be betrayed into anger or uncharitableness. Let there be no hard construction of the Divine dealings. Let patience have its perfect work. May we be willing to *do* all, and to *bear* all, for the sake of Him who hath done so much and borne so much for us. Give us a solemn sense of responsibility for every talent committed to our keeping. Let us feel that they are not given merely to be enjoyed by *us*, but to be employed for *Thee.* Alive to our stewardship, may we lay them out for Thy glory and for our own and our neighbours' good.

Bless all our beloved friends; remember them with Thy special favour:—wherever they are, may they know the true blessedness of life, when spent in Thy service. We pray for all poor afflicted ones. Ease their burdens—soothe their sorrows—dry their tears—enable them meekly to repose in Thy covenant faithfulness and love.

And now, LORD, what wait we for? our hope is in Thee. Most graciously answer us, not according to our own wishes, (often erring, often sinful,) but according to what Thou knowest would be best. We are poor and needy, yet the LORD thinketh upon us. Make no tarrying, O our GOD.

Guard us through the night. Give Thine Angels charge concerning us, that they may encamp round about us. Whether we wake or sleep, may we live together with Thee. And all that we ask is for the sake of Him whom Thou hearest always, and in whose most precious name and words we would sum up our petitions at the Throne of the Heavenly grace.

Our Father, &c.

The grace of our Lord, &c.

THURSDAY MORNING.

ALMIGHTY FATHER, Thou art from everlasting to everlasting GOD. We adore Thee as the Author of our existence, and the source of all our happiness. We desire to connect every blessing we possess with Thee;—to trace every stream of creative and providential bounty up to Thyself, the great Fountain-head. Thou alone, amid all changes, art the unchanging One. Heaven and earth shall pass away, but Thou art the same, and Thy years shall not fail.

We come, poor and needy, pleading Thine own gracious promise to give "all sufficiency in all things" to those who seek Thee. We have no offering of our own to present at Thy footstool;—we have everything to receive. There is nothing between us and everlasting destruction, but Thy mercy in JESUS. Wandering in the wilderness, in a solitary way, hungry and thirsty, our souls fainting within us, we would drink of the streams of abundant grace which flow from the Smitten Rock. These have been flowing for ages past, and yet still the warrant and welcome are free as ever. —"Ho! every one that thirsteth, come ye to the waters."

Blessed Saviour, do Thou say unto each of us, "Your sins are forgiven you." Bring us to live, more and more every day, under the constraining influence of Thy love. Being made free from sin, and having become Thy covenant servants, may we have our fruit unto holiness. May we be gaining fresh victories over our secret corruptions. May the power of evil wax weaker and weaker; and the power of Thy grace wax stronger and stronger. May we know, by joyful experience, the happiness of true holiness.

Give us reverential and child-like submission to Thy will. The lot may be cast into the lap, but the whole disposing thereof is of the LORD. Finite wisdom has no place in Thy dealings; not only are all things ordained by Thee, but ordained in ineffable wisdom and love. May the end of Thy dispensations be our growing sanctification.

Mercifully accommodate the supplies of Thy grace to the sons and daughters of sorrow. May they call upon Thee in the day of trouble, and do Thou deliver them: and though it may not be the deliverance they would have desired, may it lead them to "glorify Thee."

Look in kindness on our family circle; may Thy name be ever hallowed here; may we know the happiness of that household whose GOD is the LORD. Bless our beloved friends who may be absent from us. If separated from one another now, may we meet at last in the better country, and together enter into the joy of our LORD. Be Thou with us throughout this day. May Thy peace be upon us and upon all the Israel of GOD. Guide us by Thy counsel; strengthen us for duty; and prepare us for trial. In all our ways we would acknowledge Thee, and do Thou direct our paths. And all we ask is for the Redeemer's sake. *Amen.*

Our Father, &c.

The grace of our Lord, &c.

THURSDAY EVENING.

O GOD, Thou art great and greatly to be feared, Thy greatness is unsearchable. Heaven is Thy throne,—the earth is Thy footstool. Before Thee, cherubim and seraphim continually do cry—Holy, holy, holy, is the LORD GOD of Hosts: Heaven and earth are full of the majesty of Thy glory. Thou art the sovereign controller of all events. Thou doest according to Thy will in the armies of Heaven and among the inhabitants of the earth. The Lord reigneth. Man proposeth, but God disposeth; and He disposeth wisely and well.

We bless Thee, that as sinners we are permitted to come, with all the load of our guilt, to a great SAVIOUR. We will arise and go to our Father; we will say, Father, we have sinned against Heaven and in Thy sight,—we are no more worthy to be called Thy children! But do Thou for Jesus' sake, Thine own dear Son, have mercy upon us miserable offenders. Behold, O God, our shield: look upon us in the face of Thine Anointed. Wash us in His blood; clothe us with His righteousness: sanctify us by the indwelling of Thy Holy Spirit, and present us at last, faultless before the presence of Thy glory with exceeding joy.

May the life of JESUS be made manifest in our mortal flesh. May our citizenship be more in Heaven; may we bear upon us the lofty impress of those who are born *from* above, and *for* above,—and who declare plainly that they seek a better country.

Whatever be the sphere in which Thy good providence has placed us, may it be our earnest endeavour to use our time, and talents, and opportunities for Thee. Our season of probation must soon be finished: may we work while it is called to-day, remembering that the night cometh.

Look in kindness on Thy Church universal. Revive Thy work in the midst of the years. Return, O LORD, and visit this vineyard which Thine own right hand hath planted: may every branch be laden with fruit; found unto praise, and honour, and glory, at the appearing of JESUS CHRIST.

Compassionate the afflicted: comfort all who are cast down. Be the helper of the helpless; the refuge of the distressed; the father of the fatherless. May all mourning the loss of beloved friends be led to bow submissively to Thy sovereign will, and look forward with joyful hearts to that better time and that better world, where the fountain of these tears shall be for ever dried.

Bless each one of us now bending at Thy footstool. [May our children have Thy grace poured into their hearts. May they be defended from the snares of a world lying in wickedness. Give them to know that, if they seek Thee early, Thou wilt be found of them, but if they forsake Thee, Thou wilt cast them off for ever.] Give us all the heritage of Thy grace and love, and then we shall be rich indeed. Many are saying, "Who will show us any good?" May *we* have but one wish, "Lift Thou, upon us and ours, the light of Thy countenance." Be with us this night. It is Thou, LORD, only who makest us to dwell in safety. When we lie down to rest, let the curtain of Thy protecting providence be drawn around us, and when we awake may we still be with Thee. And all that we ask is in the name and for the sake of the LORD JESUS, in whose name and words we would further pray—

Our Father, &c.

The grace of our Lord, &c.

FRIDAY MORNING.

O GOD, our Heavenly Father, we desire, on this the morning of a new day, to encompass the footstool of Thy Throne of Grace. We thank Thee for the guardianship and care vouchsafed during the unconscious hours of sleep. Thou hast dispersed the darkness of another night, and permitted the sun once more to arise upon us. O Thou better Sun of Righteousness, do Thou disperse the deeper darkness of sin; shine on us with the brightness of Thy rising; let us enjoy this day the blessedness of peace with GOD.

LORD JESUS, we commit our temporal and eternal interests anew to Thy keeping. Soul and body are Thine by Thy redemption-purchase. May they become Temples of the Holy Ghost, with this as their superscription, "Holiness to the LORD." May nothing that is unclean or that defileth enter therein. May it be our sovereign motive, to walk so as to please Thee. May it be our heaviest cross and trial, to incur Thy displeasure. Let us not be content with a name to live. Give us grace, that we may be enabled to do Thy will and promote Thy glory;—diffusing around us, as far as we can, the influence of a holy, consistent life. In the performance of every-day duty, let us seek to make this the directory of our conduct—"How would JESUS have acted here?" May we deal tenderly with others, remembering the tenderness of Him who would not break the bruised reed, nor quench the smoking flax. May we put on, as the elect of GOD, holy and beloved, bowels of mercies, kindness, humbleness of mind, meekness, long-suffering, forbearing one another, and forgiving one another; if any have a quarrel against any, even as CHRIST hath forgiven us, so may we do also.

We pray for all in sorrow. O Thou God of all consolation, be a Father to the fatherless, a Husband to the widow, the stranger's shield, and the orphan's stay. Enable Thy suffering people to rest in Thy love—saying, The LORD'S will be done.

Bless our beloved friends; if there be any among them who are still strangers to Thee, LORD, reveal to them Thy dear Son in all His ability to save. Preserve us as a household from danger and sin; keep us in the hollow of Thy hand; and may death, when it comes, be to all of us the entrance to glory. May Thy Church universal live in the unity of the Spirit, and in the bond of peace. Revive Thy work in the midst of the years; may the day soon arrive, when all ends of the earth shall see the salvation of GOD.

We again supplicate Thy presence and blessing throughout the day. May we fall into no sin, neither run into any kind of danger, but may all our doings be ordered by Thy governance, to do that which is well pleasing in Thy sight.

Listen, gracious Father, to these our

supplications; when Thou hearest, forgive; and grant us an answer in peace, for the Redeemer's sake. *Amen.*

Our Father, &c.

The grace of our Lord, &c.

FRIDAY EVENING.

GRACIOUS FATHER, we approach the footstool of Thy throne this evening, adoring Thee as the GOD of our life and the length of our days. We bless Thee for the many tokens of Thy love daily bestowed upon us: for food and raiment—for health and strength—for friends and home—for all that brightens our pathway in life—for all that cheers and irradiates our prospects beyond the grave. LORD, how often hast Thou disappointed our fears, answered our prayers, and fulfilled our hopes; how often has Thy grace made arduous duties easy, and levelled mountains of difficulty! How often, when our hearts were overwhelmed, hast thou led us to the Rock that is higher than we; and given us help from trouble, when vain was the help of man!

We come anew to Thee this night, weary and heavy-laden, beseeching Thee to grant us the blessed sense of Thy forgiving mercy. We lament that we do not feel, as we ought to do, the burden of sin. Bring us in poverty of soul,—in self-denying, self-renouncing lowliness, to cry out, "God be merciful to us, sinners." Show us the infinite adaptation of the Redeemer, in His Person and work, to meet all the necessities of our tried and tempted natures. May His name be as ointment poured forth; may His blood be our only plea—His love our animating principle—His glory our chief end. May our souls become holy altars from which the incense of obedience ascends continually. May we be enabled to *do* Thy will and to *love* Thy will, because it is Thine. May our eye be single that our whole body may be full of light. Oh keep us from temptation; support and deliver us when we are tempted. May we be able to say, in reply to all the seductive allurements of the Evil One, "How can I do this great wickedness, and sin against God?"

Accomplish the number of Thine elect,

and hasten the coming of Thy Son's kingdom. Keep Thy churches faithful: may they earnestly contend for the faith once delivered to the saints—holding fast that which they have, that no man take their crown.

Sanctify affliction to all Thine afflicted people. Let them know that Thy chastisements are mercies in disguise; that Thou watchest every sheep in the fold; and when led out to the rougher parts of the wilderness, Thou "goest before them."

We pray for those who are living without GOD, and therefore without hope. Let them not put off until it be too late; until they are forced, with unavailing tears, to mourn wasted hours and forfeited opportunities. Convince every procrastinator that now is the accepted time,—that now is the day of salvation.

Bless us, even us, O GOD, who are now bending at Thy mercy-seat; rebuke our faithlessness — warm our love — quicken our graces:—let us live more constantly under the powers of a world to come. Ere we lie down on our nightly pillows, we would lay our sins afresh on the head of the Great Surety, that so we may retire to rest at peace with Thee; and if Thou seest meet to spare us till to-morrow, may we rise fitted for all its duties. Hear these our humble supplications; when Thou hearest, forgive; and all that we ask is for the Redeemer's sake. *Amen.*

Our Father, &c.

The grace of our Lord, &c.

SATURDAY MORNING.

MOST BLESSED GOD, who art making the outgoings of the evening and the morning to rejoice over us—we desire to begin this new day with Thee. We bless Thee for Thy sparing mercy; in having permitted us once more to lie down to sleep, and to awake in safety and comfort; may we be enabled, as dependents on Thy bounty, to receive every returning morning as a fresh pledge of Thy love.

We confess, O GOD, our unworthiness; the utter alienation of our hearts from Thyself, the source of all life and joy and blessedness. To original sin we have added manifold transgressions. Our iniquities testify against us. But we bless Thee, that where sin abounded, grace hath much more abounded. Thanks be unto GOD for His unspeakable gift; for all that JESUS died to purchase, and which He is now exalted to bestow.

O Thou Lamb of God—Thou spotless, sinless Victim—we rely on Thy most precious Sacrifice. Do Thou bear away these life-long sins of ours, into a land of oblivion, that they may rise up in judgment against us no more. LORD, may our daily walk be more circumspect and holy. Let us follow Thy will whatever it may be—though, at times, it may be at variance with our own,—feeling that the Judge of all the earth must do right, and cannot do wrong. In the spirit of Him who was "dumb before His shearers," may we have grace to say —"Even so, Father, for so it seems good in Thy sight." Above all, preserve us from the temptations of a world lying in wickedness. May we seek to walk circumspectly: remembering that our time is short; that we have much to do, and a brief time for doing it. May we have the girded loins and the burning lamps, and be like those who are waiting for their Lord's coming.

We entreat Thee to look down in

special mercy on our household — [on parents and children, masters and servants.] Visit us all with the love which Thou bearest to Thine own. [May the young be guided through the slippery paths of youth; may they be enabled early to range themselves on the LORD'S side—early to seek Thee, that they may early find Thee.] May the servants be actuated by Christian motives; — performing the duties of their calling, not with eye-service as men-pleasers, but as doing the will of GOD from the heart; may they know that in keeping Thy commandments there is a great reward. Bless those that are absent from us;— may they be shielded by Thy good providence;—make them all the children of GOD, by faith in CHRIST JESUS.

Good LORD, be with us during this day; vouchsafe us that blessing which maketh rich and addeth no sorrow with it; and when all our days are finished, do Thou receive us into everlasting habitations, for the sake of JESUS

CHRIST, our only LORD and SAVIOUR; to whom with Thee the Father, and Thee Ever Blessed Spirit, be ascribed all blessing and honour and glory and praise, world without end. *Amen.*

Our Father, &c.

The grace of our Lord, &c.

SATURDAY EVENING.

O LORD, we approach Thy sacred presence, on this the close of another day, and the termination of another week, adoring Thee for Thy great goodness. We desire, with united hearts, to set up our Ebenezer of thankfulness, and to say, "Hitherto hath the LORD helped us." We are utterly unworthy of the least of all Thy mercies. If Thou hadst dealt with us as we deserved, or rewarded us according to our iniquities, we could not answer for one of a thousand. Blessed be Thy name, Thou hast devised means by which Thy banished may not be expelled from Thee. Through the doing and dying of JESUS, the law has been disarmed of its condemning power; all its penalties have been borne; death itself has been stript of its terrors, and the Kingdom of Heaven opened to all believers.

LORD, after such a pledge of Thy

love, in not sparing Thine own Son, we believe Thou wilt with Him also freely give us all things. If Thou sendest us prosperity, may we be enabled to give Thee the return of grateful hearts, and obedient, submissive lives. If Thou deny us earthly bliss and earthly happiness, let us accept the denial as the will of Infinite Goodness. We will trust Thee implicitly. In Thee we are as secure as everlasting power and wisdom and love can make us. If there be times when we are led to exclaim—"Verily Thou art a GOD that hidest Thyself," we will look forward with joy to that better world, where mystery shall give way to perfect knowledge. LORD, make us more holy; sanctify us through Thy truth; keep us watchful; keep us humble; keep us from unchristian tempers; keep us from all pride, vainglory, and hypocrisy. Let us cultivate an habitual, realising sense of Thy Divine Presence; and in our worldly work and avocations, whatsoever we do, may we do it heartily as to the Lord and not unto men.

We pray for others as well as for ourselves. Draw near in mercy this night to any who may be in sorrow and distress, or who may be mourning the loss of beloved relatives. Do Thou sanctify their trials;—may these yield the peaceable fruits of righteousness.

Bless our beloved friends; write their names in the Lamb's book of life. Bless us who are now surrounding Thy footstool; do Thou spare us long together as an unbroken circle on earth; and when we shall be called to leave behind us this lower valley, may we be conducted into those blessed regions, which eye hath not seen, nor ear heard; where there shall be no more parting; and where we shall stand without fault before Thy Throne.

We commend ourselves to Thy Fatherly protection during the silent watches of the night. Do Thou give us tranquil repose;—may we be permitted to lie down in Thy fear, and to awake in Thy favour, fitted and prepared for the duties and services of Thy holy day. And all that we ask is for JESUS' sake. *Amen.*

Our Father, &c.

The grace of our Lord, &c.

Fourth Week.

SUNDAY MORNING.

WE will extol Thee, our GOD, O King, we will bless Thy name for ever and ever; every day will we bless Thee, and we will praise Thy name for ever and ever. We thank Thee for the return of another Sabbath. Again hast Thou permitted us to awake in safety, and not suffered our eyes to sleep the sleep of death. May it prove a holy day of rest to each of us; a rest from sin and a rest in GOD. May we welcome with gladness of heart the return of these peaceful hours. May all vain and worldly thoughts be set aside; and may we be enabled to worship Thee in the beauty of holiness.

But wherewithal, LORD, shall we come into Thy presence? Our very prayers might be enough to condemn us. Our purest services, if weighed in the balances, might rise up in judgment against us. We mourn our guilty insensibility to sin; we do not sufficiently see its vileness; we have no depressing consciousness, as we ought to have, of the plague of our own hearts; we have little realising sense of the infinite purity of Thy holy, righteous law.

We come anew in the name of Thy dear Son, confessing, and desiring deeply to feel as we confess, that we are sinners and the chief of sinners. We look to grace abounding over sin,—to infinite merit abounding over infinite demerit,—the everlasting righteousness and faithfulness of a tried Redeemer, coming in the room of our imperfections. We would place all our sins on the head of the immaculate Surety; He alone can bear them away into a land of oblivion, so that they can rise up to condemn us no more. We bless Thee that He ever liveth and reigneth for our justification. We rejoice to think of Him as our Great High Priest, with the names of His covenant people engraven on His heart, bearing them along with Him in His every approach to the throne:—that all power in Heaven and in earth is intrusted to His hands:—nothing befalls us but by His direction,—nothing is appointed us but what He sees to be for our good.

LORD JESUS, we commit our temporal and our everlasting interests to Thy keeping. We rejoice that to Thee we can confidently intrust them. Undertake Thou for us. Carry on within us Thine own work in Thine own way. Keep us from all evil that is likely to grieve us. May we know the truth of Thine own gracious promise, "As thy day is, so shall thy strength be."

We pray for all in sickness and distress; for those laid on beds of languishing; for those deprived of beloved relatives, and who are mourning those who "are not." May it please Thee to bind up their wounds, and to soothe their sorrows: direct the unwavering eye of faith to that better world, where every weight of suffering shall be exchanged for the exceeding weight of glory, and where GOD shall wipe away all tears from off all faces.

Bless our own family and friends, both present and absent. May the invisible chain of Thy covenant-love bind us all together. [Bless our children; may they be led to remember their Creator in the days of their youth, and to know that the way of holiness is the way of happiness.] Strengthen this day the ministers of the everlasting gospel; may great grace be imparted to them; may they come forth fully fraught with the blessings of the gospel of peace: and may all Thy churches, walking in the fear of God and in the comfort of the Holy Ghost, everywhere be multiplied. Promote unity and concord among Thy true people. May that predicted period soon arrive, when Ephraim shall not vex Judah, nor Judah vex Ephraim; when all shall see eye to eye and heart to heart.

Take us now under Thy care, and enable us, whether waking or sleeping, to live together with Thee; and all that we ask is for the sake of Him whom Thou hearest always; and in whose most precious name and words we would further pray—

Our Father, &c.

The grace of our Lord, &c.

SUNDAY EVENING.

MOST BLESSED GOD, whose nature and whose name is Love, we desire to draw near into Thy gracious presence on this the close of another Sabbath. We thank Thee for all the tokens of Thy mercy we have been permitted to enjoy. Abide with us, for it is toward evening, and the day is far spent. Under the realizing sense of Thy presence and nearness, we would compose ourselves to rest, with our minds stayed on Thee.

We desire anew to bless and praise Thee for Thine unspeakable gift—JESUS the Son of Thy love. There is not a ray of hope which visits our souls but emanates from His cross. He is the channel of every blessing. We rejoice to think that He is as willing as He is able to save "to the uttermost:" that at this moment He is bending upon us a gracious eye from the Throne, and, with undying and undiminished love, pleading our cause.

LORD, we come, casting ourselves on the fulness of Thy grace in Him. Sanctify us wholly, in body, soul, and spirit. Subdue our wills. Bring them in righteous subordination to Thine own. When Thou callest us to any duty, may we be ready with the response—"Here I am." May even trials and crosses become easy to us, when borne in a spirit of tranquil submission. Let us be living as pilgrims on the earth—weaned from what is uncertain and transitory here, and having our affections fixed on the things which cannot be shaken, but remain for ever. Oh that Thy love might be enthroned more than it is, as the ruling passion of our souls—and Thy glory more the end and aim of our being. May we give no sleep to our eyes nor slumber to our eyelids, till, in our hearts, we find a place for the LORD—an habitation for the mighty GOD of Jacob. Fulfil in our experience Thine own gracious promise—

"I will dwell in them and walk with them, and I will be their God, and they shall be my people."

Do Thou follow with Thine enriching blessing all the services of the sanctuary. May Thy word be quick and powerful: —forbid that impressions be suffered to die away;—do Thou fasten them as a nail in a sure place;—and may the Sabbath duties and employments diffuse their solemnity around us throughout the week.

We remember, with affectionate sympathy, the poor, the destitute, and "him that hath no helper;"—the sick—the bereaved—the dying. LORD, draw near to all such; let them know that Thou hast grace in store for their every time of need, and that there is no want to them that fear Thee. We desire for our friends Thy benediction and blessing: the LORD watch between them and us when we are absent one from another: O Thou omnipresent GOD, do Thou show that no distance can sever from

Thee,—give them every token of Thy love,—preserve them from danger,—guard them from temptation,—number them with Thy saints in glory everlasting. Bless the lambs of the flock [more especially those now before Thee] — Shepherd of Israel! make them Thine;—bringing them to the fold of grace on earth, and to Thy heaven of glory hereafter.

Bless that branch of Thy Church with which we are connected; bless Thy holy Church universal. Have mercy on those who are still sitting in darkness and in the region and shadow of death. May a lifted-up SAVIOUR, by the attractive power of His cross, draw all men unto Him.

We commend us, blessed LORD, to Thee, and to the word of Thy grace. Do Thou watch over us during the unconscious hours of sleep. May we awake in the morning in Thy favour; that so every new day being spent to Thy glory, may find us better fitted for entering on the joys of Thine everlasting Kingdom; through the merits of JESUS CHRIST, our only SAVIOUR. *Amen.*

Our Father, &c.

The grace of our Lord, &c.

MONDAY MORNING.

O GOD, Thou art the Infinite, Eternal, Unchangeable Jehovah; Thou art exalted far above our adorations and praises: angels and archangels veil their faces with their wings in Thy presence, and cry out, "Unclean, unclean!"

We acknowledge our great unworthiness; we mourn our many sins. Thy law has been set at nought by us; Thy love has been slighted; Thy Spirit grieved; Thy sovereignty disowned. We have been unmindful of Thee in prosperity—we have been prone to repine at Thy righteous ordinations in adversity. We have not endeavoured to hallow all life's duties with Thy favour. We have not sought Thy glory with singleness of eye; we have too often indulged in feelings and desires, in tempers and affections, inconsistent with our profession as followers of the LORD JESUS. Not only do our iniquities, but our best services, testify against us.

We come, casting ourselves on Thy free grace and mercy in CHRIST. We rejoice that for the greatest sins there is a great and all-sufficient Saviour. There is no load we have, but He who bore our transgression is able and willing to remove it. We will rejoice in the LORD, our souls will be joyful in our GOD, for He hath clothed us with the garments of salvation, He hath covered us with a robe of righteousness.

Enable us to walk as it becometh Thy children. Give us a holy fear of offending Thee. May we feel all sins to be grievous in Thy sight: but may it be our special desire to gain fresh victories over our besetting sins, and to be more and more fortified against the assaults of temptation. Strengthen us with might by Thy Spirit in the inner man. Make Thy grace sufficient for us, and perfect strength in weakness.

We pray not for ourselves only, but

for all whom we ought to remember at a Throne of grace. If there be any in whom we are interested who are still far from Thee, bring them nigh by the same precious blood. If any are still loitering and lingering, may they hear Thy voice, saying,—"Escape for thy life, lest thou be consumed." If there be any backsliding, LORD, reclaim them. If there be any sorrowing, LORD, comfort them. Bind up their broken hearts. Give them Thyself—the better portion which never can be taken from them. Thy way is often in the sea, and Thy path in the deep waters. But "the LORD reigneth"—may this quiet all doubts. May we wait in patience the great Day of disclosures, when "in Thy light we shall see light."

Look down in mercy on our family and household; let it be a garden which the LORD hath blessed. May we live in the unity of the Spirit, and in the bond of peace. Vouchsafe to keep us this day without sin. Be Thou our Shepherd, and we shall not want. Keep us *from*, and keep from *us*, all that would be detrimental to our souls' interests; and, when time shall be no longer, may we meet in the unclouded sunshine of Thy presence; through JESUS CHRIST, our blessed LORD and SAVIOUR. *Amen.*

Our Father, &c.

The grace of our Lord, &c.

MONDAY EVENING.

MOST GRACIOUS GOD, Father of all mercies, Thou art the KING of Kings and the LORD of Lords;—the Heaven, even the Heaven of heavens, cannot contain Thee. Myriads of blessed spirits are continually casting their crowns at Thy feet. How shall we, dust and ashes, presume to lift up our eyes to the place where Thou in glory dwellest?

Adored be Thy name for Thy free, sovereign, unmerited love in JESUS. We desire to flee to Him as our only SAVIOUR:—we *have* no other—we need no other. His finished work and complete righteousness is a glorious ground of confidence. It has been tried by countless multitudes; and the blood that has cleansed their guilty souls, has an undiminished efficacy and all-sufficiency for us.

To Thee, O GOD, we commit the keeping of our temporal and eternal interests. We cannot be in better hands than in Thine. Whether it be to *do*, or to *bear* Thy will, may it be ours meekly to say, "Even so, Father!" Whatever may most conduce to Thy glory and our good, do Thou appoint for us. Be Thou ever near us;—not as a wayfaring man that turneth aside to tarry for a night, but gladdening us with the continual sense of Thy presence and favour. Give us grace ever to recall how transient and fleeting existence is; let us feel the precarious tenure by which we hold earth's best blessings; we cannot tell what a day or an hour may bring forth. Whatsoever our hand findeth to do, may we do it with our might, remembering that there is no device, nor work, nor labour, in the grave whither we are going.

Bless all our dear friends; let them be related to Thee in the better bonds of the everlasting covenant; preserve their bodies from danger, and their souls from sin. May our household be a household of faith; may its lintels have sprinkled on them the blessed symbol of covenant love.

Bless those in sorrow; may they feel that all are "need-be" trials. Let this be their comfort in their affliction—"If we suffer with Him, we shall be also glorified together:" and let them look forward to that hour, when their sorrow shall be turned into joy; when GOD Himself shall be with them and be their GOD, and when all tears shall be wiped from off all faces.

Give each of us grace to be so living, that ours at last may be an "abundant entrance" into Thine everlasting Kingdom. Keep us waiting—keep us watching; that when the cry shall be heard in the midst of the heavens, "Behold, the Bridegroom cometh," we may be able joyfully to respond, "Even so, come, Lord Jesus, come quickly." Ere we lie down to sleep this night, renew to us the gracious sense of sin forgiven; and if spared till to-morrow, let us rise refreshed for duty, and fitted for Thy service. And all that we ask, is for the sake of Him whom Thou hearest always, and to whom with Thee, the Father, and Thee, O blessed Spirit, one GOD, be everlasting praise, honour, and glory, world without end. *Amen.*

Our Father, &c.

The grace of our Lord, &c.

TUESDAY MORNING.

ALMIGHTY and EVERLASTING JEHOVAH, Thou art the heart-searching and rein-trying GOD; Thou art of purer eyes than to behold iniquity; evil cannot dwell with Thee, fools cannot stand in Thy presence. Thou hast solemnly declared that Thou canst by no means clear the guilty. It is only because of Thy mercies in CHRIST, that we are not consumed, and that Thou hast not executed against us the cumberer's awful doom.

We bless Thee for all that JESUS hath done—for all that He is willing to do. We bless Thee that He is now exalted a Prince and a SAVIOUR;—that having purged our sins, He has for ever sat down on the right hand of GOD: and that there He must reign until He hath put all enemies under His feet. Our earnest prayer is, that each of us may be personally and everlastingly interested in His great salvation. May He be precious to us in all His offices, as our Prophet, Priest, and King; ruling over us and within us; making our hearts the habitations of GOD through the Spirit. Spare us, good LORD, spare Thy people, whom Thou hast redeemed with Thy most precious blood, and be not angry with us for ever.

Seeing Thou hast loved us with an everlasting love, may we not requite Thee with coldness and unthankfulness, —or give Thee the wrecks of 'a worn and withered affection.' May the best of our thoughts, and the best of our lives, be surrendered to Thy service. We would cast all our cares, and every individual care, on Thee; knowing and rejoicing that Thou "carest for us." Let us trust Thee in everything; let us see Thy faithfulness in every event in our chequered and changing histories. How Thou hast smoothed our way in the past! By Thee, our crosses have been lightened;

our fears disappointed, our fondest hopes fulfilled. We will trust Thee in the future. Let us feel that the great Shepherd, who gave His life for the sheep, cannot lead us wrong.

Bless our dear friends; may the LORD be their keeper; may the sun not smite them by day, nor the moon by night. Do Thou preserve them from all evil, in their going out and in their coming in, from this time, henceforth, and even for evermore.

Be merciful to the family of affliction; those laid on beds of pining sickness—those bereaved of beloved relatives. May it please Thee to help, succour, and relieve them; may they know Thine own blessed name—"The Consolation of Israel;" may they take comfort in the assurance, "the LORD will provide."

Be Thou with us throughout this day; sanctify all its duties; go with us where we go, dwell with us where we dwell: Guide us, while we live, by Thy counsel, and afterwards receive us into Thy glory. Hear us, gracious GOD, and accept of us for the Redeemer's sake. *Amen.*

Our Father, &c.

The grace of our Lord, &c.

TUESDAY EVENING.

HEAVENLY FATHER, who hast in Thy good providence permitted us to meet together this night, be pleased, of Thine infinite mercy, to vouchsafe us Thy blessing. Scatter our darkness with the beams of Thy love. Dispel all harassing thoughts, and misgivings, and disquietudes; ere we retire to rest may our souls be stayed on Thee. Unto us, O LORD, belong shame and confusion of face. We mourn that we feel so inadequately our guilt and unworthiness; that we have so little depressing sense of our alienation from Thee. We often confess with the lip what the heart does not feel. We often *appear* to be humble, when we are *not* humble,—when our hearts are full of self, and pride, and vainglory.

We desire to come anew into Thy presence, casting ourselves on the free grace, and love, and mercy of JESUS.

We rejoice that in His cross all Thine attributes have been magnified. Thou art now proclaiming to the vilest and unworthiest, that Thou hast no pleasure in the death of the wicked, but rather that he would turn from his wickedness and live. Turn Thou us, O LORD, and we shall be turned. Enable us to accept of this blessed Physician of souls, who healeth *all* our diseases. And having tasted and seen that the Lord is gracious, enable us to live as those who are not their own, but bought with a price. May we be willing to *be* anything, and to *do* anything, and to *suffer* anything for that SAVIOUR, who hath done and suffered so much for us; may our only grief be "to give Him pain"—may our "joy be to serve and follow Him." Keep us from temptation. Support and deliver us when we are tempted. Sanctify us by the indwelling of Thy HOLY SPIRIT, and bring us to live more under the influence of unseen realities.

We desire to remember before Thee

all whom we love. Hide them under the shadow of the everlasting wings, until earth's calamities be overpast. Do Thou pour Thy richest benediction on this our household. Known unto Thee are all our varied circumstances, our peculiar trials, and temptations, and perplexities. Our every burden we cast on a faithful GOD. Our souls, our lives, our cares, we leave entirely in Thy hands, saying, "Undertake Thou for us."

Pity the afflicted. Be Thou the Father of the fatherless, the Husband of the widow, the stranger's shield, and the orphan's stay; let them know that when heart and flesh faint and fail, Thou art the strength of their heart, and their portion for ever.

We now commend us all to Thy gracious keeping. The darkness of night has gathered around us; but do Thou lift upon us, O God, the light of Thy countenance:—it cannot be night if Thou art near. Watch over us during sleep, and when we awake may we be still with

Thee. We ask these, and all other blessings, trusting in the merits and mediation of JESUS CHRIST, Thine only Son, our Saviour, who with the Father and the Holy Ghost, ever liveth and reigneth, world without end. *Amen.*

Our Father, &c.

The grace of our Lord, &c.

WEDNESDAY MORNING.

GRACIOUS FATHER, Source and Giver of every good and every perfect gift—do Thou draw near to us this day in Thine undeserved kindness,—visit us with that love which Thou bearest unto Thine own.

We are receiving, morning after morning, new proofs of Thy care—new pledges of Thy mercy. Thou art loading us with Thy benefits, though we have been ungrateful and unthankful. It is in the name, and trusting in the merits of Thy dear Son alone, that we can have any confidence in approaching Thee. We rejoice that we have ever a safe shelter at the foot of His cross. We rejoice that there, every attribute of Thy nature, and every requirement of Thy law, have been vindicated and magnified. Myriads are now in glory to bear witness to the power and love of an all-gracious SAVIOUR. And what grace has done, grace can still do:—"the faithful saying" has lost none of its faithfulness. LORD JESUS, stretch forth Thy succouring hand. Save us, else we perish. There is not a sin but Thou canst cancel;—there is not the unsanctified heart which Thy promised Spirit is unable to convert into a Temple of the living GOD. Do Thou keep us from evil; preserve us from temptation. As good soldiers may we range ourselves under Thy banners; animated by holy allegiance to Him who is the great Captain of our salvation. We would seek to repose on the Divine promises. May our weakness drive us to Almighty strength. Good LORD, keep us, by Thy grace, from an uneven walk, from inconsistency of conduct. May we be gentle, and lowly, meek, and forgiving. May we overcome evil with good.

Do Thou bless this family and household. May it be one of the Tabernacles of the righteous, where the voice of joy and melody is often heard. [May the lambs of the flock be the special care of the great and good Shepherd. Blessed JESUS, seal to them early an interest in Thy covenant,—write their names in Thy Book of Life.]

We pray for all in sorrow; may they look to the hand which was pierced for them, to bind up their bleeding wounds. May He who graciously said of old, "I know their sorrows," be near, with His own exalted sympathy, to minister to their varied experiences of trial.

We pray for Thy cause throughout the world. Bless our nation; may it be the honoured instrument, among the kingdoms of the earth, in greatly promoting the glory of GOD. Bless our Queen; may she evermore have affiance in Thee, and ever seek Thy honour and glory. Bless every rank and condition; may Thy favour encompass all as with a shield.

Be Thou with us, blessed LORD, this day. May Thine angels encamp round about us and keep us in all our ways; and when we come to die, do Thou receive us into everlasting habitations, for the sake of JESUS CHRIST, our only SAVIOUR. *Amen.*

Our Father, &c.

The grace of our Lord, &c.

WEDNESDAY EVENING.

MOST BLESSED GOD, Thou hast again, in the multitude of Thy mercies, permitted us to meet together around Thy footstool. Giver of all grace, draw Thou near to us; enable us to end another day with Thee, and to retire to rest, in the conscious possession of Thy friendship and love.

What are we, that we should be permitted to approach such a glorious and infinite GOD! We are dust and ashes, —creatures of a day—who might, long ere now, have been righteously spurned from Thy presence. Blessed be Thy great and holy name, for all the manifold proofs of Thy favour. Thy ways are not as our ways; had they been so, we must all of us have perished without hope. It is of the LORD'S mercies that we are not consumed. Do thou give to each of us this night, to know the blessedness of being at peace with Thee,—of taking hold on that everlasting covenant, which is well-ordered in all things and sure; looking away from our guilty selves and our guilty doings, to Him who has done all and suffered all, and procured all for us.

Give us a deep and abiding sense of our vileness and unworthiness. May every sin which has usurped the throne of our affections be cast down, that God Himself may be our all in all. May we seek to imbibe more of the spirit, and to copy more of the example, of our Divine Redeemer. May we feel it to be our joy to serve Him, our privilege to follow Him, our sorrow to vex and grieve Him. Take us and use us for Thy glory;—sanctify our affections—elevate our desires. Keep us from being over-careful and over-troubled about earth's many things;—enable us to be more solicitous about the one thing needful; may we be covetous only of the solid and durable riches of eternity.

Bless our beloved relatives; may they

all be enabled to claim a common kindred with the one Elder Brother on the Throne. Set Thine own mark on each of them: though separated from one another now, may Thy blessed Angels gather us together, at last, in the same bundle, for the Heavenly Garner.

Let none put off preparation for death till a dying hour:—a present hour is all that we can call our own;—may we be living in that state of holy preparedness, that when the silver cord by which life is suspended is broken, we may be ushered into Thy presence, and into the enjoyment of glory everlasting.

Look down on Thy Church everywhere throughout the world;—purify her more and more;—may no weapon formed against her prosper; may her ministers be men of GOD, and may her saints and people shout aloud for joy. Do Thou satisfy Zion's poor with bread. May every afflicted one partake of Thine own consolations, and be led meekly to say, "the LORD'S will be done."

Graciously take the charge of us during this night. We commend us all to Thy fatherly protection and care;—whether we wake or sleep may we live together with Thee. And all we ask is for the LORD JESUS CHRIST'S sake. *Amen.*

Our Father, &c.

The grace of our Lord, &c.

THURSDAY MORNING.

O LORD, we desire to approach the footstool of Thy Throne, adoring Thee as the everlasting GOD, the LORD, the Creator of the ends of the earth, who faintest not, neither art weary. Thy wisdom never fails—Thy resources never exhaust. The kindness of the kindest knows a limit, but Thy kindness knows no limit. With Thy friendship, and favour, and blessing, we are rich, whatever else Thou mayest take away. Vicissitude is written on all around us—time may estrange the nearest and dearest on earth, but "Thou art the same;"—loving us at the beginning, Thou wilt love us unto the end.

We come unto Thee this morning in the name of Thy dear Son. Our sins reach unto the clouds—we cannot answer for one of a thousand; but we rejoice that we can look up to Him who *has* answered for us. Blessed Saviour, we would bury all our transgressions in the depths of Thy forgiving mercy. We *seek* no other refuge and *need* no other refuge but Thee. Relying on Thy finished work, we can look calm and undismayed on the unknown future. We can cast all our cares, as they arise, upon Thee, feeling not only that Thou carest for us, but that Thou makest these cares Thine own. We can look forward to the last enemy—to death itself, without alarm; the rays of Thy love will dissipate the gloom of the dark Valley, and cause us to rejoice in hopes full of immortality.

Meanwhile, O GOD, do Thou sanctify to us, the dealings of Thy providence. May these prove heart-searchers, quickening our footsteps Heavenward. Let us follow the leadings of the Great Shepherd of the flock. Let us repose in the blessed assurance, "we shall not want." Thou wilt not overburden us. We have known Thee in the past, we will trust Thee still.

Guide us while we live by Thy counsel, and afterwards receive us into Thy glory.

Bless Thy Church everywhere;—may all its ministers be men of God, valiant for the truth; warning every man, and teaching every man in all wisdom. Sustain the faith of those, who, amid manifold discouragements, are labouring in heathen lands: may the LORD send His Angel to stand by them, and to shut the mouth of every gainsayer. Hasten that glorious time, when the year of Thy redeemed shall come, and the whole earth shall be filled with Thy glory.

Bless all of us who are here assembled. Known unto Thee are our several wants, and temptations, and perplexities. Make Thy grace sufficient for us. May a sense of Thy presence hallow all the day's duties, and lighten all its trials. Go with us where we go: dwell with us where we dwell. May the peace of God, which passeth all understanding, keep our hearts. And all we ask is for the sake of Him whom Thou hearest always—JESUS CHRIST, our only LORD and SAVIOUR. *Amen.*

Our Father, &c.

The grace of our Lord, &c.

THURSDAY EVENING.

MOST BLESSED LORD, Father of all mercies, Thou art from everlasting to everlasting GOD; the same yesterday, and to-day, and for ever. Thou hast, in Thy great goodness, brought us again around the footstool of Thy Throne of Grace. During the past day, many of our fellow-beings have gone into eternity; —we are spared. Thou hast been compassing our path—shielding us from danger, and guarding us from temptation. None is so able, none is so willing, as Thou art, to befriend and guide us in every perplexity. We can experience no real blank, and mourn no real loss, if we have *Thee.* The LORD liveth, and blessed be our Rock, and let the GOD of our salvation be exalted.

We desire this night to retire to rest, in the assured confidence of Thy favour. Forgive all the sins of the past day—its sins of omission and commission,—of thought, and word, and deed;—whatever has been inconsistent with Thy pure and holy will. Make us more zealous for Thy honour and glory;—may we maintain a constant and habitual hatred of those sins which have so long severed us from Thee. May we ever be near the atoning fountain;—continually hidden in the clefts of the Rock; that when the last summons shall come, our end may be peace.

Bless all who are in affliction. May they be led to lean confidingly on the arm of JESUS, and they shall be more than conquerors.

We pray for a whole world. Pity the nations that are sunk in heathen darkness. Hasten the Pentecostal effusion of the latter day. When the enemy is coming in like a flood, may the Spirit of GOD lift up a standard to resist him. Bless all Thy faithful missionaries. In lands where Christian sanctuaries are not, be Thou a little sanctuary to all Thy true servants;—may they know Thee, as a prayer-hearing, a prayer-answering, a covenant-keeping God. Direct their hearts into Thy love, and into the patient waiting for CHRIST.

Bless our household. [Parents and children, master and servants.] May the joy of the LORD be our strength. May we feel that in keeping Thy commandments there is a great reward. As the pillar of cloud goes before us by day, may the pillar of fire be with us by night. May angels gather around us during the unconscious hours of sleep;—may no danger befall us, and no plague come nigh our dwelling. If pleased to spare us till to-morrow, may we rise fitted and prepared for all the duties to which we may be called.

And now unto Him who alone is able to keep us from falling, and to present us faultless before the presence of His glory with exceeding joy, to the only wise God and our Saviour, be ascribed all blessing and honour, dominion and praise, world without end. *Amen.*

Our Father, &c.

The grace of our Lord, &c.

FRIDAY MORNING.

ALMIGHTY and MOST MERCIFUL FATHER, Thou art great and greatly to be feared; Thy greatness is unsearchable. Thou art infinite in wisdom, and power, and love; Thy justice is as the great mountains, Thy judgments are a great deep.

LORD, our hearts are deceitful above all things and desperately wicked. We have done those things we ought not to have done, and we have left undone those things which we ought to have done, and there is no health in us. Have mercy upon us, for His sake, in whom Thou seest no iniquity. We have nothing of our own but our sins; all that is good in us comes from Him; we would confidently repose our everlasting interests on His finished work.

Forbid that we should presume on Thy mercy,—that we should take encouragement to sin from abounding grace. May we feel that Thy pure eye is upon us; that Thou triest us, not according to man's fallible judgment, but according to the standard of unerring rectitude and holiness. May it be our lofty aim to be the servants of righteousness; may we show that the influence of Thy goodness and loving-kindness is to lead us to repentance,—to reclaim our hearts from their wanderings, and bring them into captivity to the obedience of JESUS. We desire to take Him in all things as our pattern. When in want of direction or guidance in any duty, or under any perplexity, may this be ever our inquiry —How would the SAVIOUR have acted here? May we imbibe His unselfish spirit. May life be a more constant effort than it has been, to crucify self and to please GOD. Let us be willing to accept of anything with Thy approval, and to dread nothing but what incurs Thy wrath and displeasure. In our varied spheres may we seek to feel that we have *some* work to perform—*some* talent to trade on. Let us cast by faith our mites into Thy treasury, that we may earn at last this Thine own meed of approbation,—" They have done what they could."

Let Thy hand be around all our beloved friends, present or absent. Inscribe their names in the Lamb's Book of Life; may they be Thine on that day when thou makest up Thy jewels. Sanctify sorrow to the sons and daughters of affliction; let them not murmur under Thy Fatherly chastisements; let them own Thy Sovereignty, and take comfort in the thought that Thou doest all things well; seeing no hand but Thine in the bestowing and removing the gifts of Thy bounty. " The LORD reigneth, let the earth be glad."

We commend us, blessed LORD, to Thee, and to the word of Thy grace. Do Thou hear, answer, and accept of us, for the sake of Him whom Thou hearest always, and to whom, with Thee, the Father, and Thee ever blessed Spirit,—

Three in One in covenant for our Redemption,—be ascribed all blessing, and honour, and glory, and praise, world without end. *Amen.*

Our Father, &c.

The grace of our Lord, &c.

FRIDAY EVENING.

O LORD, we desire to approach Thy Throne of Grace, thanking Thee for the liberty of access we at all times enjoy into Thy presence. We bless Thee that the gates of prayer are ever open;—that Thou regardest the cry of the needy, and never sayest unto any of the seed of Jacob, "Seek ye my face in vain."

How unworthy are we to come to Thy footstool. There is enough of coldness in our prayers, of insincerity in our repentance, of imperfection in our best attempts to serve Thee, that were we tried by these, we must have perished for ever. Our prayers themselves require forgiveness.

Blessed JESUS, Thou great covenant Angel, let down Thy golden censer into the midst of us this night, that we may have these our petitions perfumed with the incense of Thine adorable merits. In Thee alone are our persons and our services rendered acceptable. We flee to the foot of Thy cross. Here we are safe, though everywhere else we be in danger. Let us exercise a simple confidence and trust in Thy completed work. We bring every sin to Thy atoning blood—every wound to Thy healing. May we have Thee *in* all, and *for* all the duties and difficulties and trials of life. Do Thou disarm all its crosses—sanctify its losses: —may prosperity and adversity be alike used for Thy glory.

Let us hate evil;—give us to feel how cherished sin ruins our peace, and unfits us for the enjoyment of Thee and Thy service. Keep us especially from presumptuous sins, let them not have dominion over us. Loving Thee our GOD, may we love our fellow-men; may we be patient and unselfish, forbearing and forgiving, lowly and meek, pitiful and courteous. Let us overcome evil with good. May all our things be done with charity. May we show, by our Christ-like walk and conversation, what spirit we are of; not conformed to the sinful practices and base compliances of a world lying in wickedness,—but seeking to have our conduct moulded in conformity with Thy holy will.

Thou sympathising SAVIOUR, be the Friend of the friendless; the support and solace of the bereaved. There are nameless sorrows on earth which are beyond the reach of the tenderest human sympathy — Blessed JESUS, make them Thine. This is Thy sublime prerogative —"I know their sorrows." Let all Thy tried people with joy anticipate that gladsome morning, when the shadow of death shall be merged in eternal glory.

Bless our beloved friends;—may Thy loving eye rest upon them; may a sense of Thy favour pervade all their doings. May none be found wanting at Thy right hand, on the Great Day.

Let us seek to order our plans as dying creatures. Night after night, as we retire to rest, may we think of that deeper darkness, which must, sooner or later, gather around us. Shepherd of

Israel, who never slumbers and never sleeps, be Thou very near us. As we now retire to rest, may we repose in Thy keeping; and in the morning, when we rise, may we rise refreshed for duty,—fitted for whatsoever may be in store for us.

Hear us, blessed GOD, and grant us an abundant answer, for the sake of Him whom Thou hearest always. *Amen.*

Our Father, &c.

The grace of our Lord, &c.

SATURDAY MORNING.

O LORD, we desire to come into Thy blessed presence on this the morning of a new day, adoring Thee for all Thy mercies. Last night we might have slept the sleep of death; we might have been startled by the midnight cry, "Prepare to meet thy GOD!" But Thy love and forbearance again permit us to meet on praying ground; the day of grace is lengthened, and the GOD of grace waits to be gracious.

LORD, we look back with amazement at Thy patience. Mercies have been abused—providences slighted—warnings neglected. Our lives contain a long retrospect of ingratitude and guilt:—Justly mightest Thou have said, "Let them alone"—"why should they be stricken any more?"

But Thou art not willing to leave us in our state of estrangement and sin. Thou art ever opening up a way for the return of Thy prodigal and wayward children. In wrath Thou art remembering mercy. We have still the richest encouragement to repair to the opened fountain; Jesus still waits—His blood still cleanses—His spirit still pleads. The faithful saying is as faithful as ever —"Him that cometh unto me I will in no wise cast out." Thy thoughts are not as man's thoughts. Had they been so, the sinner, with all his deep depravity, and unutterable vileness, and base ingratitude, would not have been thus welcomed, pardoned, accepted, *loved.*

We desire to receive this new day as a fresh gift from Thee. Let Thine approval form, throughout it, a holy incentive to every duty. Let us feel that we never can be happy but when pleasing Thee. Let us be aiming at a conquest of self; subordinating all we do to Thy will and service. Keep us from alienating existence from its great end, by living to ourselves. We look to Thy grace to enable us thus to will and to do. Thou hast wrought all *for* us, and Thou alone canst work all *in* us. Strengthen us with might by Thy Spirit in the inner man. How slow we are to believe that our truest security is leaning confidingly on Thine arm. Thou art faithful that promised. Thy name is the GOD of *all* grace; Thou givest all sufficiency in *all* things. The cup runneth over that is filled by Thee—and nothing can come wrong to us that comes from Thy hand.

Bless all near and dear to us: all that is truly good for them, in this life, do Thou bestow; and, what is better, do Thou give them the heritage of glory. [May our children grow up as willows by the water-courses, and be a seed to serve Thee when we are gathered to our fathers.]

Take us all, young and old, this day under Thy protection. God of all mercy, spread Thy covering wings around us. Be our GOD and Guide even unto death, and finally bring us to Thine everlasting kingdom, through the merits of Thy dear Son — our only LORD and SAVIOUR, who, when He was on earth, taught us thus to pray, saying—

Our Father, &c

The grace of our Lord, &c.

SATURDAY EVENING.

O LORD, Thou art the King eternal, immortal, and invisible. The Heaven of heavens cannot contain Thee. Myriads of pure and holy spirits cease not day nor night to celebrate Thy praises. All their adorations cannot add to Thy glory, or augment Thy blessedness.

What are we, that we should be permitted to approach the presence of a GOD so great and so glorious, and who is of purer eyes than to behold iniquity? *We* are apt to palliate sin; but no sin is trivial with *Thee*. We are apt to forget sin, we are too willing to hide it from Thee, and to hide it from ourselves; but we cannot evade Thy righteous scrutiny. We cannot screen our guilt from the Great Heart-searcher:—all things are naked and open unto the eyes of Him with whom we have to do.

But blessed be Thy name, though Thou

art the Greatest and the Holiest of all Beings, Thou art also the kindest and most forgiving. Who is a GOD like unto our GOD, that pardoneth iniquity! Sinners and the chief of sinners, we can find rest and peace in the work, and merits, and righteousness of Thy dear Son. Confiding our eternal all to Him, we can rejoicingly say—Return unto Thy rest, O our souls, for the LORD hath dealt bountifully with us.

Bring us to live more constantly and habitually under the constraining influence of Redeeming love. May these souls of ours, ransomed at such a price, be dedicated to Thy service. Forbid that any of us should be content with a name to live, if we are dead; and deceive ourselves with the form of godliness. Let us know, more and more, that this is Thy will concerning us, even our sanctification. May we grow in grace. May the struggle against corruption issue in the confirmed habit of a holy life. May Thy Spirit—

the Spirit of grace, and peace, and love—dwell in our hearts, and elevate our affections. Keep us from pride—the master-passion of our fallen and corrupted natures; from vain-glory and hypocrisy; from envious, uncharitable, unforgiving frames and tempers. Keep us from the secret atheism which refuses to own Thy hand, and which regards as "accident" that which is the sovereign and deliberate decree of a Wisdom which cannot err. Oh, may we be preserved in body, soul, and spirit; ready to be presented at last faultless before the presence of Thy glory with exceeding joy. We would desire especially, as the week is closing, to remember before Thee all our beloved friends. God of all grace, dispense to them Thy richest blessings. May those ties which on earth are so precarious and liable to be dissolved, be rendered indissoluble by grace; that so, when we part on earth, it may be only to meet in glory everlasting.

Have mercy on all who are in affliction.

O Thou healer of the broken-hearted, Thou helper of the helpless, may every wounded spirit be bound up by Thee. May the lonely and unbefriended feel, that in the loneliest solitude, they are not alone, if Thou, their GOD and Father, art with them. Spare valued and valuable lives; and may those who are appointed to death, have the valley-gloom lighted with Immanuel's love.

And now, LORD, what wait we for? Our hope is in Thy mercy. Be Thou with us this night. Be the Guardian of our unconscious hours. Whether we wake or sleep, may we live together with Thee. Our wishes, our desires, our interests, our joys, our sorrows, our friends, we leave entirely to Thy care and disposal. Prepare us for the solemn duties and services of another day of the Son of man. Give to all of us a double portion of Thy Holy Spirit, that our souls may be fitted for holding nearer and more intimate fellowship with Thee. And all that we ask is for the sake of Him who is the Resurrection and the Life, and who with the Father and the Holy Spirit, ever liveth and reigneth, world without end. *Amen.*

Our Father, &c.

The grace of our Lord, &c.

Occasional Prayers.

MORNING OF A COMMUNION SABBATH.

ALMIGHTY AND EVERLASTING GOD, we bless Thee for the return of another day of the Son of man. Pour out upon us a double portion of Thy grace;—fill our hearts with Thy love. May all vain, and wandering, and sinful thoughts be repressed; may our communion and fellowship this day be with the Father, and with His Son JESUS CHRIST.

We thank Thee for the prospect we have of anew commemorating the dying love of our risen and exalted Redeemer; —of surrounding once more the table in the wilderness, and partaking of the bread of everlasting life. Give to each of us the "wedding garment." Let us prepare to meet our GOD. May we feel that the place whereon we are to stand is holy ground; and rejoice at the renewed opportunity of testifying, in the presence of angels and men, our unaltered and unalterable attachment to our blessed LORD and Master. In a strength greater than our own, may we be enabled to resolve, that He will be henceforth ours only—ours wholly—ours for ever.

Give us this day lively apprehensions of the great love wherewith He hath loved us. May these dead and lukewarm souls of ours be quickened into newness of life. May our faith be invigorated, and our love deepened, and our graces strengthened. May this be the grateful aspirations of all our hearts—"What shall we render unto the LORD for all His benefits towards us? We will take the cup of Salvation, and call upon the name of the LORD; we will pay our vows unto the LORD now in the presence of all His people."

We pray for all who are to receive along with us this day the sacred emblems. Give to each of them some special tokens of Thy covenant love. May they see the King in His beauty. May their experience be—"It was good for us to draw near unto GOD." Keep back all presumptuous and unworthy guests. Encourage all misgiving, trembling, faint-hearted ones. While feeling their own *un*worthiness, may they remember they go to commemorate the infinite *worthiness* of Him who is *All-worthy*. May they hear Thy voice of encouragement saying, "Fear not, for I know that ye seek JESUS who was crucified."

Go forth this day everywhere with the preaching of Thy holy Gospel. May wanderers be reclaimed; may mourners be comforted; may saints be edified; may Thy name be glorified. Stand by Thy ministering servants:—may they hear the sound of their Master's footsteps behind them:—may they hide themselves behind their LORD, pointing away from the excellency of their own speech and their own wisdom, to Him, who alone, by the attractive power of His Cross, can draw all men unto Him.

We commend to Thy paternal keeping our beloved friends. May they be among the number of Thy sealed ones. Sanctify them in body, soul, and spirit, that they may at last be presented faultless and unblameable before Thy dear Son at His appearing. Bless this household; masters and servants [parents and children.] Let us all at last sit down, one united and undivided family, with Abraham, and Isaac, and Jacob, at the better feast of communion in Thy heavenly kingdom. And all that we ask is for the sake of Him, in whose most precious words we would further pray, saying,

Our Father, &c.

The grace of our Lord, &c.

EVENING OF A COMMUNION SABBATH.

MOST GRACIOUS GOD, who hast in Thy good providence brought us to the close of another Sabbath, we entreat Thee to accept of our unfeigned thanks for all the loving-kindness and tender mercy Thou hast made this day to pass before us. We bless Thee for all that our eyes have seen, and our ears have heard, and our hands have handled, of the Word of life. Do Thou wash us after supper. May the benediction and blessing of the Master of the feast rest upon us. May we descend the holy mount rejoicing in the presence of Him who brought us into His own banqueting house, and caused His banner over us to be love. Give us grace to pay the vows which our lips have this day uttered; fulfil in us all the good pleasure of Thy goodness, and the work of faith with power, that the name of the LORD

JESUS CHRIST may be magnified. As we have named His precious name anew, may we henceforth depart from all iniquity. Send us help out of Thy sanctuary, and strengthen us out of Zion :—may the LORD grant us the desires of our hearts, and fulfil all our petitions. May a Communion Sabbath's services diffuse a hallowed glow over all the duties and engagements of the week :—may we show to the world that we have been with JESUS, and that it has been no vain thing for us to draw near unto GOD.

LORD, our own strength is weakness; we cannot follow out one single resolution, depending on ourselves. We will go in the strength of the LORD GOD. May we be kept by Thy mighty power. May we exercise a holy jealousy over our hearts. Let us hear Thy monitory voice ever saying to us,—"When thou thinkest thou standest, take heed lest thou fall." Keep us from the beginnings of sin; preserve us from venturing on debateable ground; may we ever be where we should wish to be found by our LORD when He cometh. Our cry would be "More grace! more grace!"—our trust would be in that GOD who, as the GOD of *all* grace, can impart an *all*-sufficiency in *all* things. Sanctify our hearts by the indwelling of Thy blessed Spirit. May they become temples dedicated to Thy glory. May this be their motto and superscription—"Holiness to the LORD."

We pray for those who may have joined with us this day in the same solemn and sacred ordinance. We commend each and all to the great Shepherd of the sheep, who, through the blood of the everlasting covenant, will make them perfect to do His will.

Regard, in Thy great mercy, any who may have been prevented from waiting upon Thee in Thy house and in Thine ordinances. May they that tarry at home divide the spoil. Compensate, by an increased supply of Thine own promised grace, for the want of public services. Transform every sick-chamber, and every death-bed, into the house of GOD and the gate of heaven. May valuable lives be prolonged. May the bereaved be comforted: may they repose on Him who *bare* their sorrows and who *knows* their sorrows.

Take the charge of us this night; watch over us during the unconscious hours of sleep; may we all come at last to the eternal blessedness of an uninterrupted Communion Sabbath in glory, around which no shadows shall fall;—for "there shall be no night there, and they need no candle, neither light of the sun, for the LORD GOD giveth them light, and they shall reign for ever and ever." *Amen.*

Our Father, &c.

The grace of our Lord, &c.

PRAYER FOR A DAY OF HUMILIATION.

ALMIGHTY AND MOST MERCIFUL GOD, Thou art glorious in holiness, fearful in praises, continually doing wonders. Thou art of purer eyes than to behold iniquity;—Thou canst not look upon sin but with abhorrence. Do Thou pour out upon us this day the spirit of grace and of supplication—the spirit of humility and deep abasement. In self-renouncing lowliness we desire to take the publican's place and cry out, "Unclean, unclean!—GOD be merciful unto us sinners!"

Father! we have sinned against heaven and in Thy sight, we are no more worthy to be called Thy children. Our sins have reached unto the clouds: they are highly aggravated;—they have been committed against manifold privileges, solemn warnings, earnest entreaties, innumerable mercies. The kindness of the best earthly friend has been nothing to Thine. Morning and evening have had the same testimony to bear, of unmerited patience, and condescension, and love:—and yet our hearts have been ungrateful and unthankful. They have been mercies abused—warnings slighted—providences unsanctified.

We acknowledge our sins as *individuals*. Our hearts have been estranged from Thee;—we have been lovers of pleasure more than lovers of GOD. Divine things have not been exercising a paramount influence over us. We have been living for earth;—seeking our chief good short of Thyself, the only soul-satisfying portion. Our love has been cold—our faith weak—our graces languid—our services polluted; self and sin have mingled with our best attempts to glorify Thee. We have not been exercising a holy watchfulness over ourselves. We have been guilty of envy and jealousy;—we have harboured unkind suspicions of others;—we have not had that charity which hopeth all things, and believeth all things, and endureth all things. In prosperity, we have been unmindful of the Author of our mercies. In adversity we have been tempted to give way to hard thoughts and unrighteous surmises about the faithfulness and rectitude of Thy dealings.

We acknowledge our sins as *families*. We have not been exhibiting consistency of walk. Thy Word has not been prized as it ought. The flame of love and devotion has not burned brightly on the domestic altar as it ought. The leaven of vital godliness has not been pervading, with its hallowed influences, our family engagements, and occupations, and duties. We have not done what we might have done for Thee;—we have been more set on selfish and worldly schemes and objects, than on devising measures for the promotion of Thy glory and the good of our fellow-men. The religion professed by the lip has not been verified and exemplified by holy and devout practice.

We confess our sins as a *church* and as a *nation*. LORD, Thou hast filled our cup with mercies—Thou hast dealt with us as Thou hast not dealt with any other people. But, alas! have we not abused our privileges? We mourn and blush to think of the vice and profligacy—the intemperance and ungodliness, which is rising up in terrible memorial against our land. We mourn our desecrated Sabbaths, and deserted sanctuaries, and unread Bibles; —we mourn the eye-service and the lip-homage which, too often among Thy professing people, takes the place of heart and soul consecration:—we mourn the little we have done, the much we have left undone, to promote Thy cause in the world. Father, forgive us these our many and heinous offences: humble us in the dust because of all our unworthiness. Give us grace this day, while we mourn the past, humbly, but earnestly, to resolve to live more devotedly to Thee in the future. Accept of our unworthy confessions, for JESUS' sake. Sprinkle these guilty hearts with His precious blood. Let us seek, in all time to come, to walk before Thee in holiness and righteousness of life, to the glory of Thy holy name.

[IF ON A DAY OF HUMILIATION PRECEDING THE COMMUNION.]

(In the prospect of sitting down at Thy holy table, may we be enabled to look upon Him whom all these transgressions of ours have pierced, and to mourn. May we be melted under a sense of our own great unworthiness, and of His amazing love. When we take into our hands the memorials of His anguish and sufferings, may they read to us an affecting lesson of the evil of that accursed thing, which cost the Son of GOD so much. Let us not venture on that holy ground with one sin unrepented of, or uncrucified. Let us go, humbly resolving that we are to be wholly Thine;—that whatsoever others do, as for us, we will serve the LORD.)

[IF ON THE OCCURRENCE OF ANY NATIONAL CALAMITY—SUCH AS PLAGUE, PESTILENCE, FAMINE, OR WAR.]

(Thou art now seeing meet in Thine adorable providence, to read aloud to us, as a nation, solemn lessons of rebuke and judgment. We acknowledge anew that our sins are the fruitful cause of national calamities. Instead of wondering at these vials of Thy wrath, we have rather reason to wonder and be amazed that Thou hast forborne so long—that Thou hast been so slow to deal out merited retribution. LORD, listen to our fervent supplications for Thy returning favour; avert further calamity. Let us fall into the hands of GOD, for great are His mercies. Do Thou say to the destroying angel, as He is even now hovering around us, "It is enough, stay now thine hand." May this national chastisement lead to national repentance. May we come forth from the furnace purified as the gold—vessels of glory more and more meet for the Master's use.)

We commend ourselves and all belonging to us to Thy care and keeping—never leave and never forsake us; and all that we ask or hope for, is in the name and for the sake of JESUS CHRIST, our blessed LORD and SAVIOUR. *Amen.*

Our Father, &c.

The grace of our Lord, &c.

CHRISTMAS DAY.

ALMIGHTY AND EVERLASTING GOD, the Father of our LORD JESUS CHRIST, we desire, on this sacred anniversary, to draw near, in His name, to Thy footstool. Our souls would magnify the LORD—our spirits would rejoice in GOD our SAVIOUR; for He that is mighty hath done great things for us, and holy is His name. Blessed be the LORD GOD of Israel, for He hath visited and redeemed His people, and hath raised up for us an horn of salvation in the house of His servant David.

We look back with gratitude and joy to that memorable night, when the angels appeared over the Plains of Bethlehem, proclaiming that the promised Child was born, the promised SAVIOUR was given; —that through Him, while glory was secured to GOD in the highest, peace was proclaimed on earth, and good-will to the children of men. We adore the amazing condescension which brought the LORD of life and of glory from His Throne in Heaven to that manger of humiliation; "God over all," dwelling in union with an infant of days!

We desire to present ourselves before the Holy Child JESUS, like the wise men of old, with the gold, and frankincense, and myrrh of our best affections and deepest love. Had it not been for this inconceivable stoop from the infinite to the finite, where would we have been this day? Well may we join in the angelic song, and say, 'Glory! eternal glory be to God in the highest, for His best—His unspeakable gift; without which, not one ray of hope or joy could have visited our doomed world.' As we gather in thought around His cradle, may our souls rise in lively gratitude to Him who spared not His only Son, but freely gave Him up unto death for us all. We will sing unto the LORD a new song, for He hath done marvellous things; His right hand and His holy arm have gotten Him the victory. Thanks be unto GOD who giveth us the victory, through the LORD JESUS CHRIST.

May we seek, by holy, righteous, and consistent lives—by holy living and holy walking—to show that we are not insensible of all His unmerited love and kindness. Blessed JESUS, make us Thine. Sanctify us wholly:—wean us from earth:—train us for glory. Forbid that it should be said, that for any of us, Bethlehem's manger was prepared in vain, and Bethlehem's angel-song sung in vain. Contemplating Thee this day in Thy humiliation, when Thou wast made in the likeness of man, may it be ours to look forward, with holy joy, to Thy second coming in the clouds of Heaven—Thy tears, and sorrows, and sufferings all past;—when the Babe of Bethlehem—the sufferer of Gethsemane—the crucified of Calvary—shall be seated on the Throne of universal empire, and crowned "LORD of all."

We pray that Thy holy name may be

everywhere magnified. Arise, O GOD, and plead Thine own cause. May a dark world be soon cheered by the wondrous proclamation we this day love to recall. May the "Prince of Peace" take to Himself His great power and reign;—causing men to beat their swords into ploughshares and their spears into pruning hooks.

We pray for the afflicted:—lead them too this day to Bethlehem's SAVIOUR:—show them all that He was willing to do for *them;* and may this reconcile them to bear patiently whatever trial He may see meet to appoint; may they rejoice in His tender sympathy, remembering one great end for which He descended to the lowly manger was—that *in all points* He might be tempted even as they are.

Bless our family—we would seek to avouch the LORD this day to be our GOD. Whatever others do, as for us we will serve Thee. [Bless our children—let them be brothers and sisters of Him who (once the lowly Child JESUS) is now an exalted Elder Brother on the Throne.]

Give us all that is really good for us; —withhold all that is evil. May Thy will be our only rule and directory; may we trust Thee in everything; and look forward with joyful hearts to that better time, when we shall be permitted, with a multitude which no man can number, to take up the song of this day, and ascribe "glory to GOD in the highest," for that mercy which, through His own dear Son, is to endure for ever. And all we ask is for His sake. *Amen.*

Our Father, &c.

The grace of our Lord, &c.

THE LAST NIGHT OF THE YEAR.

O LORD, we adore Thee as the GOD of times and seasons, of days, and of years. Thou alone art without any variableness or shadow of turning. Thou didst inhabit the glories of eternity, before the birth of time or of worlds. Thou hadst no beginning of days;—Thou canst know no end of years. Amidst fleeting moments and revolving seasons, the past and present and future are, to Thee, one ever-present "Now." A thousand years in Thy sight are but as yesterday when it is past, or as a watch in the night. It is our comfort to know, amid so much that is transient in a fleeting world, that *Thou* art the same,—that Thy Throne has the pillars of immutability to rest upon,—that though all be changing and hastening to decay and dissolution, "*Thy* dominion endureth throughout all generations."

We desire, on this the last day of

another year, to bow at Thy footstool, and to take a solemn retrospect of all the year's mercies. We have indeed good reason this night to set up our Ebenezer, and to say, "The LORD hath helped us." It is a retrospect of love. We may well write as our motto on its waning hours, "We have received at the LORD'S hands double for all our sins." From how many unseen dangers hast Thou delivered us;—from how many temptations, which we had no strength of our own to resist, hast Thou rescued us! How many during this last year have been wasted with sickness, or racked with pain, or stretched on beds of languishing; yet Thou hast mercifully protected us. [How many households have been darkened with the shadows of death—the hallowed circle broken, and yet we are all still among the living to praise Thee.] How many thousands of our fellow-men, since the year began, have passed into eternity; but we, unworthy cumberers, are yet spared;—the axe has not been laid to the root of the tree;—we are preserved another year longer;—night after night we laid ourselves down and slept because the LORD sustained us, and we are still the objects of Thine unceasing watchfulness and tender care.

O GOD, when we think of Thy great mercies, what shall we say of the retrospect of our past sins? The record of another year is now ascending to Thy Throne; alas! it is the record of abused kindness, and despised warnings, and misimproved providences, and lukewarm hearts, and careless, thankless lives. Were we to be judged by the duties and doings, the sins and shortcomings of any one day of the passing year, we would be righteously condemned. Oh, ere the record *has* passed upwards to Thy Great Book, do Thou wash out every stain in the blood of Immanuel. We have no hope but in Him. We desire this night to hear His own blessed words of consolation and mercy—"Son, daughter, be of good cheer, your sins are all forgiven you." We lament, O GOD, how little we have been affected by all that He hath done for us. Lead us to repentance. Bring us more and more to realise the depth of obligation under which we are laid to Him who hath loved us with an everlasting love. We would mourn the past, and seek for "more grace" for the future. Come, LORD, search us and try us, and see if there be any wicked way in us, and lead us in the way everlasting. May the lives which Thou hast, during another year, prolonged and preserved by Thy bounty, be willingly consecrated as thank-offerings to Thy praise.

We desire, at this time more particularly, to commend to Thy Fatherly care and goodness all in whom we are interested. May our absent friends meet us this night in spirit around the Throne of the heavenly grace, severally commending *us*, as we now desire to commend *them*, to Thy care and love. Make them the objects of Thy providential bounty, and the subjects of Thy heavenly grace and kingdom. May they too be brought to bewail the sins of the past, and seek for new grace in entering on a new period of existence. Oh, when this rapid flight of years and seasons shall have come to an end, may we all be found in the regions of everlasting day, to unite together in singing the song of Moses and of the Lamb.

Compassionate all in affliction; may the bereaved be comforted,—may the dying be prepared for their great change,—may the living know that they too must die.

We desire to retire to rest under the solemnising impression that we are a year nearer eternity,—that a year more of our probation time is fled,—that a year less of grace and opportunity and privilege belongs to us. LORD, take the charge of us; and if Thou art pleased to spare us to see the light of a new day and a new year, may it be to us the emblem of a better morning and a nobler term of being, when earth's shadows and darkness shall have for ever fled, and when we shall be satisfied, awaking in Thy likeness. And all we ask is for the REDEEMER'S sake. *Amen.*

Our Father, &c.

The grace of our Lord, &c.

FIRST MORNING OF A NEW YEAR.

ALMIGHTY AND EVERLASTING GOD, Thou art the Alpha and the Omega—the First and the Last. Amid all the vicissitudes of a changing world, Thou changest not. All things below must perish—but Thou remainest the same.

Thou hast mercifully preserved us to see the commencement of another year. We desire to begin this new period of our existence by consecrating its hours to Thee. Before we enter on its manifold duties, and its unknown trials, we beseech Thee to impart to us Thy gracious benediction;—we would seek to connect its coming blessings with Thee,—to own Thy hand and Thy wisdom in its coming sorrows; we would seek to feel that it can only be to us a *happy* year by being a *holy* one—spent in Thy service and devoted to Thy praise.

It is one of the many new years we

have seen; we cannot tell how few we may have yet to see. Our prayer is, that we may live this year as if it were to be our last.

LORD, we desire to begin the year, where we would wish to begin and to end its every day—at the opened Fountain. We desire to take as our motto and superscription throughout its course—"GOD forbid that we should glory, save in the Cross of the LORD JESUS CHRIST." We desire to connect this new year's morning with the great atoning sacrifice, without which no years could have revolved to us. Our every temporal comfort, as well as every spiritual blessing, flow to us entirely from JESUS. Oh, do Thou enkindle in our hearts a flame of more ardent devotedness to Him, whose amazing love it is that crowneth every year with goodness, and makes all its paths to drop fatness. Good LORD, we desire, this morning, to make a fresh consecration of ourselves and our household unto Thee. Sprinkle our lintels with the blood of the everlasting covenant. Set Thine own seal and mark on our foreheads. If in past years there has been forgetfulness of Thee—if Thy kindness has been abused, and Thy mercies slighted, and Thy name dishonoured, enable each and all of us to make this year one of more undivided surrender to Thy service. May it be a new year of love, and meekness, and forgiveness, and close walking with GOD. May sin be more dreaded, and holiness more loved. May the lessons of eternity come more powerfully and impressively home to us. Let us live as immortal beings. Let us live a dying life. Let it not be the impression of a solemn anniversary like the present, but an habitual conviction—"The fashion of this world passeth away." O LORD, accept of this our united new year's sacrifice. We would light our flickering lamps at Thy holy altar; do Thou plenish them day by day with the oil of Thy grace;—that should any of us be summoned in the course of the year to meet our LORD, we may not have to make the mournful confession—"Our lamps have gone out."

Good LORD, bless all our dear friends; we would remember *them*, as we trust they are remembering *us*, this day, at Thy footstool. Hear our mutual prayers: may the cloud of mercy descend on all our heads. Though absent from one another on earth, may faith bring us near, by having our tents pitched by the gate of heaven.

Bless our native land; may it ever remain a centre of holy influences—distinguished by that righteousness which exalteth a nation. Bless our Queen, our rulers, our senators, our magistrates. Bless the ministers of the everlasting Gospel; may they be wise to win souls; and may every religious privilege we now enjoy, be handed down unimpaired to the latest posterity.

God of all grace, we commend us to Thee: undertake Thou for us. Let the pillar of Thy presence go before us. Do

Thou direct, control, suggest throughout this year, all that we design or do,—so that every power of our bodies, and every faculty of our souls, may unite for the showing forth of Thy praise and glory. And all that we ask is for the sake of JESUS, Thine only Son and our SAVIOUR. *Amen.*

Our Father, &c.

The grace of our Lord, &c.

FOR A TIME OF BEREAVEMENT.

O LORD GOD ALMIGHTY, we rejoice to think that "the LORD reigneth;"—that though Thy way may sometimes seem to be in the sea, and Thy path in the deep waters, and Thy judgments unsearchable, yet that nothing can happen by accident or chance—but all is the unerring dictate of infinite wisdom and unchanging faithfulness and love.

Where would we be at this hour, but for the blessed assurance, "*This* also cometh from the LORD of Hosts," who, though "wonderful in counsel," is ever "excellent in working." Often we cannot discern, through our tears, the rectitude and love of Thy varied dispensations—often are we led to say, with trembling and misgiving hearts, "Verily, Thou art a GOD that hidest Thyself." But "all is well;" we could not wish our concerns in better hands than in Thine; may this wondrous challenge silence and rebuke every murmur,—"He that spared not His own Son, but delivered Him up for us all, how shall He not with Him also freely give us all things?" Thou canst not send one trial that is unnecessary, or light one spark in the furnace that might be spared. We will be dumb, we will open not our mouths, because *Thou* didst it. Man *may* err, and *has* often erred; but, O unerring GOD! Thy faithfulness Thou hast established in the heavens;—the Judge of all the earth *must* do right. We would seek to lie submissive at Thy feet, and say in unmurmuring resignation, "Thy will be done." We "*fear* to enter into the cloud,"—Thou hast afflicted us by terrible things in righteousness; the desire of our eyes has been taken away by a stroke;—the shadows of death have unexpectedly fallen around us! Oh forbid that we should rebel under the rod, and refuse to be comforted. Let us glorify Thee "in the fires;" let us feel that if we are Thy children, there is not a drop of wrath in that cup of sorrow; but all is love, infinite love. We would see no hand but Thine: "the *LORD* gave us our blessings, and the *LORD* has a supreme and inalienable right to take them away"—"Even so, Father, for it seemeth good in *Thy* sight."

Our earnest prayer, blessed God, is, that this severe trial may be sanctified to us all; we have need of such a blow to remind us that earth is not our rest. We were leaning on the creature—we were disowning and undeifying the Great Creator. Thou wouldst not leave us to ourselves, to settle on our lees. Thou sawest the need of fatherly chastisement to bring back our alien and truant hearts to Thyself. Oh, may we listen to our Father's voice; may we feel it to be a *loud* voice, and yet full of gentle tenderness; may it rouse within each of us the question, "What wilt Thou have me to do?" May we "arise and call upon our GOD." Thus may this very affliction, which, for the present, seemeth not to be joyous but grievous, nevertheless afterward yield the peaceable fruit of righteousness.

LORD, abundantly sanctify this solemn dispensation to every member of our household,—to all friends and neighbours. May the monitory voice sound loudly in our ears, "Be ye also ready." It is another testimony borne to the truth, that at such a time as we think not, the Son of GOD may come. May it be ours ever to live in preparation for that solemn event which awaits us all. Whatsoever our hand findeth to do, may we do it with our might, remembering that there is no work, nor device, nor labour, nor repentance in the grave, whither we are going.

Sprinkle us all with the blood of JESUS; give us all a saving interest in Him, as the Resurrection and the Life. Let us hear His voice of encouragement and love, sounding amid the stillness of the death-chamber, and from the depths of the sepulchre, "Fear not: I am He that liveth and was dead, and behold I am alive for evermore, and have the keys of the grave and of death." "Yet a little while, and He that shall come will come, and will not tarry;" soon shall these bitter tears and partings of a weeping world be over; death-divided friends shall meet, never again to know separation. Enable us to look forward to that blessed hope and that glorious appearing, when "them also which sleep in JESUS will GOD bring with Him."

LORD, meanwhile descend, and to the friendless prove a Friend. O Thou Helper of the helpless, Thou Comforter of all that are cast down, Thou better and dearer than the dearest and best of earthly relatives, give us that grace which Thou hast promised specially in seasons of weakness; may we realise the truth of Thy own precious promise, "As thy day is, so shall thy strength be." Deep is now calling tc deep, all Thy wáves and Thy billows are going over us; yet the LORD will command His loving-kindness in the day-time, and in the night His song shall be with us, and our prayer to the GOD of our life. However low we may be sunk under the waves, the arms of Thy love and upholding grace are lower still. May it be our sweet experience, that the deeper we sink, only discovers more the infinite depths of Thy love and mercy. May this thought reconcile us to bear all and suffer all—'we shall soon be done with a present evil world, and be with our GOD, and that for ever and ever.'

Do Thou hide us meanwhile in the clefts of the Smitten Rock, until this and all other of earth's calamities be overpast. May we trust Thee where we cannot trace Thee; and wait patiently for the Great day of disclosures, when *all* shall be revealed, and *all* be found redounding to the praise and the glory of Thy great name.

Hear us, blessed GOD; and all that we ask is for the sake of Thy dear Son, our only LORD and SAVIOUR. *Amen.*

Our Father, &c.

The grace of our Lord, &c.

PRAYER TO BE USED BY A FAMILY DETAINED FROM PUBLIC WORSHIP.

ALMIGHTY AND EVERLASTING GOD, Thou art glorious in holiness, fearful in praises, continually doing wonders. Thy Kingdom is an everlasting Kingdom, Thy dominion endureth throughout all generations. Amid all the changes and vicissitudes of a changing world Thou the LORD changest not. Thou art the same, and Thy years shall have no end.

We desire to bless and praise Thy holy name for the return of another day of the Son of man. This is the day which the LORD hath made, we will rejoice and be glad in it. Do Thou go forth everywhere with the preaching of the everlasting gospel. Clothe Thy priests with salvation: let Thy saints shout aloud for joy. May the assemblies of Thy people be enabled to worship Thee in the beauties of holiness, and feel it to be good for them to draw near unto GOD. It is our comfort to know that Thou art not confined to temples made with hands; — that wherever there is a true worshipper, *there*, there is a prayer-hearing GOD. O Thou GOD of Bethel—GOD of our fathers, and the covenant GOD of all who truly fear Thee, do Thou look down in kindness on us who are prevented this day, by the restraints of Thy Providence, from joining with our fellow-Christians in the public services of the sanctuary. It is not to numbers Thou lookest: —wherever two or three are gathered together in Thy name, we have Thine own recorded promise, that there Thou wilt be in the midst of them to bless them and to do them good. Though Thou lovest the gates of Zion, Thou art not forgetful of the dwellings of Jacob. Thou hast said that Thou wilt create upon every dwelling-place of Mount Zion, as well as upon her assemblies, a cloud of smoke by day, and the shining of a flaming fire by night. Let the pillar of Thy promised presence go before us; may we feel like Thy disciples of old, when the voices of heavenly messengers on the mount were silenced—that we are "alone with Jesus." Gracious SAVIOUR, abide Thou with us; we are independent of all ordinances if we have Thee. It is Thy presence and love which gives a blessing to all outward means of grace; Thy most hallowed altar is the altar of a humble, lowly, contrite heart; Thy most acceptable sacrifice is the incense of grateful love—of devoted, obedient, submissive lives. O Thou Great Angel of the everlasting covenant, do Thou sprinkle these our unworthy prayers and services with the incense of Thy spotless merits, that thus, worthless and polluted in themselves, they may be made acceptable in the sight of GOD.

LORD, may every returning Sabbath be finding us better prepared for the eternal Sabbath.—May sin be dying within us. May we be progressively advancing in the divine life. May we be abounding in faith, and hope, and love; seeking by Thy grace to walk in newness of life—more humbly—more consistently, more prayerfully. May we live as dying creatures.—May all the solemn events that are taking place among ourselves and around us, be so many voices proclaiming, "Arise and depart ye, for this is not your rest." LORD, break the world's alluring spell; strip it of its vain fascinations; let the "seen and the temporal" be more subordinated to the "unseen and the eternal;"—may we give evidence to all, that we are living under the power and influence of gospel principles and renewed affections. May we be meek and gentle—patient and forbearing—thankful and resigned. And even though trial and sorrow should at times be our allotted portion, may we seek to show that the grace of GOD can impart an inner sunshine which no outward darkness can obscure.

Do Thou look down in mercy on all our dear friends;—may they too see the good of Thy chosen, and glory with Thine inheritance;—may the fragrance of this day's services follow them throughout the week;—may they have the increasing experience that the way of holiness is the way of happiness.

Bless all Thy missionary servants. Give them a double portion of Thy Spirit.—May it be their privilege this day to gather in some sheaves of the great gospel harvest.—May the LORD of the harvest stand by them to strengthen them; should they be now only sowing in tears, may it be theirs, at last, to reap in joy.

And now, LORD, what wait we for? Our hope, for ourselves, and for all near and dear to us, is in Thee.—Hear us for the sake of Him whom Thou hearest always, and in whose most precious name and words we would further pray, saying,

Our Father, &c.

The grace of our Lord, &c.

FOR ONE IN DANGEROUS ILLNESS.

O GOD, our Heavenly Father, in Thee we live, and move, and have our being. We rejoice to think that Thy hand is never shortened, that it cannot save—that Thine ear is never heavy, that it cannot hear. We thank Thee for Thine own recorded promise, that the prayer of faith, if consistent with Thy blessed will, will save the sick. We entreat Thee to look down in great mercy on that member of our family who is this day laid on a bed of languishing. May it please Thee of Thine infinite goodness speedily to restore [him.] Do Thou rebuke [his] disease. Bring him back from the gates of the grave. May this sickness not be unto death, but for the glory of GOD, that the Son of God may be glorified thereby. Mitigate the severity of pain. Grant [him] patience under [his] sufferings, unmurmuring submission to the will of Him who afflicteth not willingly. [His] times are in Thy hands. We commend [him] soul and body to Thee, the great Physician. If Thou seest meet to raise [him] up, may restored health and strength be more than ever given unto [him]; but if Thou hast otherwise determined, do Thou fit [him] for [his] eternal change. To [him] to live may it be CHRIST—to [him] to die may it be great gain.

PRAYER TO BE USED AT THE BEDSIDE OF A DYING BELIEVER.

EVER BLESSED GOD, we rejoice to know that our times are in Thy hands. The LORD gives us our lives—the LORD has a sovereign right to take them away; give us grace to say, 'Blessed be the name of the LORD!' Do Thou look down in great mercy on Thy servant, whom Thou art about to take to Thyself. Let [him] know, that, leaning on JESUS, the sting is plucked away from death, and the grave is robbed of its victory. Oh, Thou ever-living Redeemer, Thou great "Abolisher of Death," who hast brought life and immortality to light by the Gospel, smooth this dying pillow,—let Thy voice be heard, saying, "Fear not, it is I; be not afraid!" Grant relief from suffering. Give [him] a peaceful entrance into glory: may Thine angels even now be waiting to waft [him] to Thy presence—

may [he] know that Thou art faithful who hast promised, "Lo, I am with you alway, even unto the end of the world!" Forgive, oh, forgive all [his] past sins. May this be the one glorious truth to which [his] soul clings in a dying hour —"The blood of JESUS CHRIST, GOD'S Son, cleanseth from all sin." LORD, may Thine own blessed soul-sustaining peace be [his];—a few more moments and [he] will wake up in heaven, —sorrow and sighing shall have fled away for ever. May [he] feel that to depart and to be with CHRIST is indeed far better. Hear us, good LORD, for JESUS' sake. *Amen.*

"And I heard a voice from heaven saying unto me, Write, Blessed are the dead which die in the LORD from henceforth: Yea, saith the Spirit, that they may rest from their labours; and their works do follow them."

"In my Father's house there are many mansions; if it were not so, I would have told you. I go to prepare a place for you; and if I go to prepare a place for you, I will come again and receive you unto myself, that where I am there ye may be also."

"When thou passest through the waters I will be with thee; and through the rivers, they shall not overflow thee: when thou walkest through the fire, thou shalt not be burnt; neither shall the flame kindle upon thee. For I am the LORD thy GOD, the Holy One of Israel, thy SAVIOUR."

"Yea, though I walk through the valley of the shadow of death, I will fear no evil, for Thou art with me, Thy rod and Thy staff they comfort me."

"For we know that if our earthly house of this tabernacle were dissolved, we have a building of GOD, an house not made with hands, eternal in the heavens."

"And one of the elders answered, saying unto me, What are these which are arrayed in white robes? and whence came they? And I said unto him, Sir, thou knowest. And he said unto me, These are they which came out of great tribulation, and have washed their robes, and made them white in the blood of the Lamb. Therefore are they before the throne of GOD, and serve Him day and night in His temple: and He that sitteth on the throne shall dwell among them. They shall hunger no more, neither thirst any more; neither shall the sun light on them, nor any heat. For the Lamb which is in the midst of the throne shall feed them, and shall lead them unto living fountains of waters: and GOD shall wipe away all tears from their eyes."

THE END.

Printed by BALLANTYNE, HANSON & Co.
Edinburgh & London

By Mrs. PEARSALL SMITH,

Author of "The Christian's Secret of a Happy Life."

THE UNSELFISHNESS OF GOD, AND HOW I DISCOVERED IT. Large crown 8vo, 6s.

OLD TESTAMENT TYPES AND TEACHINGS. Crown 8vo, 5s.

EDUCATE OUR MOTHERS; or, Wise Motherhood. Crown 8vo, 1s.

EVERY-DAY RELIGION. The Common-Sense Teaching of the Bible. Crown 8vo, 2s.; cloth limp, 1s. 6d.; paper cover, 1s.

"Passages of Scripture are brought together in a manner that marvellously illuminates the subjects discussed; and the expositions are most clear in thought and apt in illustration."—*Life of Faith.*

THE CHRISTIAN'S SECRET OF A HAPPY LIFE. By H. W. S. Revised Edition. Small crown 8vo, paper cover, 1s.; cloth limp, 1s. 6d.; cloth, 2s.; with gilt top, 2s. 6d.; cloth, gilt edges, 3s.

"Full of bright and cheering thoughts."—*Church Bells.*

"A book that is capable of doing untold good in the way of promoting a more entire surrender of the soul and consecration to the will of God."—*Rock.*

THE CHRISTIAN UNDER REVIEW.

A Series of Works on Practical Christian Life.

Small crown 8vo.

THE CHRISTIAN'S INFLUENCE. By the Ven. William Macdonald Sinclair, D.D., Archdeacon of London. 2s.

THE CHRISTIAN'S START. By the Very Rev. the Dean of Norwich. 1s.

THE MORAL CULTURE OF THE CHRISTIAN. By the Rev. James McCann, D.D. 1s.

THE PATHWAY OF VICTORY. By the Rev. Robert B. Girdlestone, M.A., Hon. Canon of Christ Church, and late Principal of Wycliffe Hall, Oxford. 1s.

THE CHRISTIAN'S DUTIES and RESPONSIBILITIES. By the Very Rev. the Dean of Norwich. 1s.

THE CHRISTIAN'S AIMS. By the Rev. Alfred Pearson, M.A., Incumbent of St. Margaret's Church, Brighton. 1s.

THE INTELLECTUAL CULTURE of the CHRISTIAN. By the Rev. James McCann, D.D. 1s.

THE CHRISTIAN'S PRIVILEGES. By the Rev. W. J. Deane, M.A. 1s.

THE CHRISTIAN'S INHERITANCE. By the Rev. C. A. Goodhart, M.A., Incumbent of St. Barnabas', Highfield, Sheffield. 1s.

"We dipped into these pages alike with pleasure and profit. The writers, each on his own theme, seem steadfastly to keep in view scriptural teaching, sound doctrine, and the trials and temptations which beset the daily life and walk of the believer."—*Word and Work.*

By the Rev. GEORGE EVERARD, M.A.

MERRY AND WISE. Talks with Schoolgirls. Pott 8vo, 1s.

FIGHT AND WIN. Talks with Lads about the Battle of Life. Pott 8vo, 1s.

LINED WITH LOVE. Friendly Talks with Young Girls about the Yoke of the Lord Jesus. Pott 8vo, 1s.

IN SECRET. A Manual of Private Prayer. 16mo, 1s.

"IN THE MORNING." A Scripture Prayer and a Meditation for each Morning in the Month. 16mo, 1s.

"IN THE EVENING." Thirty-one Scripture Promises with a Meditation for Every Evening in the Month. 16mo, 1s.

THE SHIELD, THE SWORD, AND THE BATTLE. Crown 16mo, 1s.

YOUR SUNDAYS. Fifty-two short Readings, especially intended for Schoolboys. Crown 8vo, 2s. 6d.

THE BELLS OF ST. PETER'S, and other Papers on Gospel Truth. 16mo, 1s.

YOUR INNINGS. A Book for Schoolboys. Crown 8vo, 1s. 6d.

HIS STEPS: Traced in the Great Biography. Crown 8vo, 1s. 6d.

THE RIVER OF LIFE; or, Salvation Full and Free, 16mo, 1s.

STRONG AND FREE. A Book for Young Men. 16mo, 1s.

BRIGHT AND FAIR. A Book for Young Ladies. 16mo, 1s.

FOLLOW THE LEADER. Counsels on the Christian Life. 16mo, 1s. 6d.

DAY BY DAY; or, Counsels to Christians on the Details of Every-day Life. Cheap Edition. 16mo, 1s. 6d.

NOT YOUR OWN. Counsels to Young Christians. 16mo, 1s.

LITTLE FOXES: And How to Catch Them. 16mo, 1s.

MY SPECTACLES: And What I Saw with Them. 16mo, 1s.

BENEATH THE CROSS. Counsels, Meditations, and Prayers for Communicants. 16mo, 1s.

SAFE AND HAPPY. Words of Help and Encouragement to Young Women. With Prayers for Daily Use. 16mo, 1s.

By the Very Rev. DEAN FARRAR,

THE HERODS. Crown 8vo, 3s. 6d.

TEMPERANCE REFORM. Crown 8vo, 1s. 6d.

SIN AND ITS CONQUERORS. Small crown 8vo, 1s. 6d. cloth.

WOMAN'S WORK IN THE HOME: As Daughter, Wife, and Mother. Long fcap. 8vo, cloth, 1s. 6d.; paper cover, 1s.

"Consists of three delightful sermonettes or essays in Dr. Farrar's happiest style. They are so eloquent; the allusions are so apt and picturesque; they are so full of humanity kept in its proper place by humour which hardly shows on the surface."—*Literary World.*

"The book is an excellent one."—*Glasgow Herald.*

THE YOUNG MAN MASTER OF HIMSELF. Long fcap. 8vo, 1s. 6d. cloth.

By Mrs. A. RUSSELL SIMPSON.

FRIENDS AND FRIENDSHIP. Demy 16mo, 1s.

BUILDING FOR GOD; or, Houses not Made with Hands. With Illustrations. Square 16mo, 1s.

STEPS THROUGH THE STREAM; or, Daily Readings for a Month. Square 16mo, 1s.

BEAUTIFUL UPON THE MOUNTAINS. Square 16mo, 1s.

WELLS OF WATER. Chapters Descriptive and Practical of the Wells mentioned in Scripture. Square 16mo, 1s.

GATES AND DOORS. Square 16mo, 1s.

A PITCHER BROKEN AT THE FOUNTAIN. Royal 32mo, 3d.

NISBET'S MINIATURE CHRISTIAN CLASSICS.

Red Line Editions. Crown 16mo. Uniformly bound in cloth, 1s. each; with gilt edges, 1s. 6d.; half bound, gilt top, 1s. 6d.; paste grain, 2s. 6d. each.

1. BOGATZKY'S GOLDEN TREASURY.
2. KEBLE'S CHRISTIAN YEAR.
3. THE IMITATION OF CHRIST (THOMAS À KEMPIS).
4. THE POEMS OF GEORGE HERBERT.
5. BUNYAN'S PILGRIM'S PROGRESS.
6. THE DIVINE INDWELLING. Selections from Writings of WILLIAM LAW. With Introduction by Rev. A. MURRAY.

By the Rev. J. R. MACDUFF, D.D.

BRIGHTER THAN THE SUN. A Life of our Lord for the Young. With twelve Full-page Illustrations. Post 8vo, 3s. 6d. Cheaper Edition, paper cover, 1s. ; cloth, 2s.

THE BOW IN THE CLOUD ; or, Words of Comfort for Hours of Sorrow. Royal 32mo, 1s.

THE MORNING AND NIGHT WATCHES. In one Vol. 16mo, 1s. 6d. ; separately, 1s. each.

SUNSETS ON THE HEBREW MOUNTAINS. With Frontispiece. Post 8vo, 3s. 6d.

MEMORIES OF BETHANY. With Frontispiece. Crown 8vo, 3s. 6d.

STRENGTH FOR THE DAY. A Daily Book in the Words of Scripture for Morning and Evening. With an Introduction. 16mo, 1s. 6d.

THE GATES OF PRAYER. A Book of Private Devotion for Morning and Evening. 16mo, 1s. 6d.

FOOTSTEPS OF ST. PAUL. Being a Life of the Apostle. Designed for Youth. With Illustrations. Crown 8vo, 5s.

By MATTHEW HENRY.

EXPOSITION OF THE OLD AND NEW TESTAMENTS. With Practical Remarks and Observations—

In Nine Volumes. Imp. 8vo, £2, 2s.
In Six Volumes. Medium 8vo, £1, 11s. 6d.

By the Rev. E. W. MOORE, M.A.,

INCUMBENT OF EMMANUEL CHURCH, WIMBLEDON.

CHRIST IN POSSESSION; or, The Yielded Life. Crown 8vo, 2s. 6d.

THE CHRIST-CONTROLLED LIFE; or, The Secret of Sanctity. Fourth Edition. Crown 8vo, 2s. 6d.

"An admirable little book."—*Word and Work.*

"It is enough to say that the intensity and reality of conviction which have made Mr. Moore's spoken utterances so forceful and so fruitful are found here; and better still, there is also the quickening touch of an anointed servant."—*Life of Faith.*

"Sensible, simple, and earnest."—*Christian Leader.*

THE SPIRIT'S SEAL Crown 8vo, 2s. 6d.

By the Rev. J. R. MILLER, D.D.,

Author of "Making the Most of Life," &c. &c.

GLIMPSES THROUGH LIFE'S WINDOW. Small crown 8vo, with Portrait. Gilt top, 2s. 6d.

GIRLS: FAULTS AND IDEALS. With Quotations from Girls Letters. Crown 8vo, 6d.

YOUNG MEN: FAULTS AND IDEALS. With Quotations from Young Men's Letters. Crown 8vo, 6d.

www.ingramcontent.com/pod-product-compliance
Lightning Source LLC
LaVergne TN
LVHW010218110826
845151LV00004B/1135
9781425526399